FLINGS, FROLICS, *and* FOREVER AFTERS

FLINGS, FROLICS, *and* FOREVER AFTERS

{ A SINGLE WOMAN'S GUIDE TO **ROMANCE AFTER FIFTY** }

Katherine E. Chaddock &
Emilie Chaddock Egan

TEN SPEED PRESS
Berkeley | Toronto

Ten Speed Press
Box 7123
Berkeley, California 94707
www.tenspeed.com

Distributed in Australia by Simon and Schuster Australia, in Canada by Ten Speed Press Canada, in New Zealand by Southern Publishers Group, in South Africa by Real Books, and in the United Kingdom and Europe by Airlift Book Company.

Cover and text design by Catherine Jacobes
Front cover and page ii image, *Adam and Eve* by Peter Paul Rubens, used courtesy of The Bridgeman Art Library/Getty Images.

Library of Congress Cataloging-in-Publication Data

Chaddock, Katherine E.
  Flings, frolics, and forever afters : a single woman's guide to romance after fifty / Katherine E. Chaddock and Emilie Chaddock Egan.
      p. cm.
  Summary: "A guide to dating men for women over fifty looking for friendship, sex, or long-term commitment"--Provided by publisher.
  Includes bibliographical references and index.
  ISBN-13: 978-1-58008-716-2
  ISBN-10: 1-58008-716-7
1. Dating (Social customs) 2. Mate selection. 3. Middle aged women. I. Egan, Emilie Chaddock. II. Title.
  HQ801.C425 2005
  6467'7'0844--dc22

                              2005013456

Printed in the United States of America
First printing, 2005

1 2 3 4 5 6 7 8 9 10 — 09 08 07 06 05

To all my best girlfriends and best guy friends. You have been essential to the laughter, the love, and the learning.

—KATHERINE

With all my love to Don, who met a laughing, joyful girl at a party, asked her to dance, and remained by her side while she became a wife and a mother.

And to Steve, who met a grieving widow at a party, asked her to dance, and remained by her side while she became a laughing, joyful girl once again.

And also to Casey, who walked loyally by my side during my darkest hours and kept me safe.

—EMILIE

Contents

Acknowledgments

From Katherine: Who knew that with more than half a century of life experience I would still need the assistance and support of scores of others in producing this book? To those who contributed their memories, suggestions, advice, and applause, I will remain grateful throughout my next half century of experience. A big hug to my women friends whose experiences supplied the ideas that initially inspired this volume. An air kiss to men friends whose expert and/or inept relationship abilities confirmed the need for such a book.

I especially thank my very best girlfriend, my daughter Adrienne, and my most indispensable man, my son Brett, for their amazing belief in a mother who still can't figure out the buttons on her DVD remote. Everlasting gratitude to Emilie, for hanging in, and to Emilie's family for hanging in with her.

My friends, associates, interviewees, and others whose information and encouragement have been invaluable throughout this project include: longstanding friends Lisa, Cathy and Larry, Barbara, Linda T., Linda J., Beverly, Cathy and Blake, Debby, Franci, Teri, Helen, Bob B., Bob T., Bill and

Janis, Janet and Mike, Claudia, Teresa K., Alan, Jim, Tom, Susie, Michele, and the rest of the gang from Washington, D.C., Utah, South Carolina, and beyond; tennis pals Pam, Laurie, Karen, Delores, Teresa, Cindi, Beverly, Bene, Jean, Jeanie, Nancy, Jo, Dana, and the entire Q.V. tennis team; newer, but equally crucial, friends Iris, Gail, Susan, Lois, Mary, Bev, Bob S., Linda E., Chris, Philo, John, Amy, Jana, Jack, Michelle, Rhonda, Mike, John, Fred, Mary Adair and Ron, Carolyn and Bill M., Carolina and Bill R., Brenda, and Elizabeth. To the men of various brief and long romantic connections, I toss a wink and a nod for ego boosting and ego busting in fairly equal measure. You know which fits you.

~

From Emilie: I first send all my love and gratitude to my wonderful family: my children, who make life worth living; Christina, Alexandra, Matthew and his wife Angela, and Jenny and her husband David and their darling boys Emmanuel Donald and Raoul William; also to the rest of the family: Katherine, Adrienne, and Brett; and to Bob, Tracy, Fiona, and Lucy.

Second, I send a sincere thank you to all the good women friends from throughout the years and across the miles: Ceil, Betty, Patti, Karen, Penny, Terry, Patti, Carol, Susan, Penelope, Barbara, Judy, Peggy, Leah, Pam, Joy, Rae, Lu, Sandi, Susie, Sandra, Candy, Dorothy, Sally, Jana, Gina, Karla, Barbara, Eleanor, Susan, Sandy, Judy, Mickey, Betty Ann, Ellen,

Madeleine, Lucy, Mary, Ginny, Marianna, Elaine, Liz, Karin, Myriam, Jean, Susan, Ann, Marilyn, Mary, Gay, Nancy, Sue, Caryn, Holly, Bonnie, Jerry Anne, Gay, Jan, Kathy, Lois, Marie, Penny, Nikki, Jane, Beth, Pam, Suzy, Jenny, Trixie, Pam, Suzi, Nancy, Jenny, Fran, Sheila, Sheryl, Maureen, Maxine, Barbara, Suzanne, Jane, Marie, Millie, Diane, Linda, Martha, Eileen, Suzy, Ann, Helen, Linda, Diane, Cathy, Deborah, Genevieve, Julianne, Anne, Sally, Annie, and especially Joan, whose example gave me strength. May we always be "girls" in spirit.

Together, we send a bouquet of gratitude to the first true believer in this work, Adam Chromy of Artists and Artisans, Inc., whose faith we could not manage to shake as we tested his patience and humor. A very big bow of appreciation goes to our editor, Julie Bennett, and all the others at Ten Speed Press who helped nudge this book into reality. To our readers—all those silver and sexy fifty-something ladies—heartfelt thanks for being women who inspire us just because we know you are out there.

Commit to Action

From Double Whammy
to Double Wow

*F*IFTY-PLUS AND SINGLE. Thankfully, that phrase does not describe your dress size or your lifestyle as a hermit supporting twenty-three cats. It more accurately depicts your experience and independence—the status that gives you a mandate to shape your own life. You've figured out a lot of once-worrisome unknowns about your work, your home, your family, and your friends. You've discovered that you can replace your toilet tank float and fire your gynecologist. You've learned that you can still giggle with the girls and ogle the guys.

Yes, the guys! They are out there, and very much on your mind. They can be fun companions or enduring partners. They make you feel alive, fascinating, happy, romantic, lovely, and loved. Or not. If they are not in your orbit, not paying attention, or simply not your type for either a friendship or romance, "not" becomes a discouraging reality. Single women beyond the half-century mark report that fewer and fewer mature men are available, or interested, or free of personality disorders. We wrote this book so you can turn that situation around. We drew from our own experiences with divorce, widowhood, and the single life after fifty, as well as the experiences of women in similar circumstances throughout the country, to discover the steps that lead to good times and good romance. We found the common threads of collective, winning know-how that provide support, ideas, and a plan of action for women seeking satisfying relationships with men.

Based on our experience and others' success stories, we developed an eight-step plan to help single women over fifty find and enjoy men, from guy pals to romantic partners. While we present specific suggested actions you can take within each step, we urge you to adapt our guidance to your own style and preferences. A planning guide at the conclusion of step 8 encourages you to put in writing the actions you will take—actions that follow the eight steps, but are tailored to your own circumstances. You'll notice that everything about the steps we suggest and the actions you take require you to commit to *movement.* Nothing happens while you are sitting still. Languishing is out; energetic action is in. You get up, get out, get going, and get the guy. If you think you are too old, too unhappy, too timid, or too uncertain, we say take action anyway, even if you have to start with one very small step today, two tomorrow, and three the next. When you change your stuck-in-your-tracks behavior, your attitude will fall in line. And attitude is key to energizing yourself into movement, which in turn will lead you to a satisfying, joyful life. You will soar with the eagles!

It Happens to Us (and It Will Happen to You)

There's no getting around it: turning fifty was a bit of a setback for each of us. But only a bit. Katherine stayed in bed late on her birthday and read Erica Jong's rollicking take on the milestone in *Fear of Fifty*. Emilie went shopping and danced the night away at a big party. We had health, energy, and optimism going for us; and we were each comforted by the realization that fifty was our age, not our IQ. Besides, we weren't exactly broadcasting our ages to a lot of people. Our husbands knew and didn't seem to mind, and our kids were easily sworn to secrecy.

Little did we know that these birthdays marked the beginning of the decade of the double whammy. Emilie was soon to become a widow, Katherine was soon to divorce. Suddenly we weren't just fifty-something women. We were fifty-something *single* women. The difference was daunting.

First, you come unglued. Even if you were never married and okay about it, the milestone creates a disquieting sense of aloneness. Then, maybe in a few months or a few years, you are surprised to realize that you are, in fact, still living. You've licked your wounds, done your mourning, paid your therapist, and waded through the self-help books re-gifted from friends once in similar circumstances. You notice that there is a light at the end of the tunnel, and it is not a train hurtling toward you. Unfortunately, neither is it a lantern on the hard hat of a craggily handsome train engineer determined to guide you out of the darkness. At this point you finally come to the unexpected conclusion that the rest of your life is likely to include actually having a life, and that you, and only you, can shape that life.

A Man Is Still a Man

For most of us, having a life includes fulfilling relationships with men. We have plenty of good times ahead, and satisfying male-female relationships will only make them better. Even if we don't want to make a long-term commitment, we enjoy having the laughs, the shoulder pats, the companionship, and the ego boosts that men can provide. The men we converse with, share meals with, walk the beach with, share a home with, or even marry have a nice way of making us feel good. This simple fact doesn't change with age, even in close company with the other reality that these same men sometimes have a way of making us feel lousy.

We each began to seek out our next relationships with men very slowly, emerging from our cocoons of shock cautiously at the urging of friends who cared enough to teach us what they had learned. Their instruction became the foundation for the steps we are now able to share with you in a succinct, waste-no-time way. For Emilie, the process meant coping with the sentiments of three grown children who sainted their good father and reserved a room in a convent for their mother with the wandering eye. As Emilie managed to move beyond grief and share time with men despite the disapproval of her brood, she found that the process could be adolescent and silly, but really quite fun. It eventually led to a special commitment with a terrific guy. Katherine confronted her newly single state by refusing to meet new men but deciding to exhume every old boyfriend (available or not) she could locate. After some amazing nonrelationships with those of the old gang who passed themselves off as somewhat interested, she became more open to making new acquaintances. Eventually she found herself having a terrific time with several male friends, both old and new.

But Let's Get Real ...

While the relationship-seeking urge clearly recycles itself through the years, what does appear to change with age is our ability to find the guy, initiate a romance, or capture a commitment. It seemed so much easier in our more youthful years. This, of course, makes perfect sense. There are more than ten million of us single American women beyond the fifty-year mark, while there are only about seven million unattached men in that age group. The odds can look dismal. They get worse when we consider that among those seven million, you will find thousands each of:

- **The Bubble Boy:** If he appears insensitive, it's only because he has no real feelings. Don't even bother trying to get through to him.

- **The Desperado:** He's so needy you need a backhoe to fill his every desire.

- **The Lone Ranger:** Alone but not lonely, he's a cowboy at heart who will ride off into the sunset without you every time.

- **The Freeloader:** He lights at the locale of his best return on investment. You invest time and energy, but he expends little emotional capital.

- **The Terminal Case:** It might be about his never-ending grieving or his waning physical health. In any case, don't be his nurse with a purse.

- **The No-Brainer:** He seemed like a ten at first, but that was the age at which he stopped maturing.

Subtracting these nonstarters whittles our field of dreams down to about four million men—maybe five million, if we consider those smart guys in their thirties and forties who are willing to romance older women. That calculation gives us about half a guy each. For single siblings like us, that means we'd have to do battle over who gets the head and who gets the heat, and nobody should have to make a decision like that.

You Will Beat the Odds

Don't get discouraged. You need only find joy and romance with one or several of the four or five million men in your general population. Even bad odds are not insurmountable. They just mean you need to think smart, work hard, and *get going right this minute.*

If this seems easier said than done, that's why we wrote this book—to give you the eight-step process you need to succeed with the men who will enrich your life. You are not stuck in imaginary superglue that binds you to your current neighborhood, your long-time employer, your aging family members, or your twenty-nine-year-old son who has come home to camp out while figuring out his next career move. You have options and opportunities that reflect your energy and optimism. Single at fifty-plus is a path in the sun, not a dead-end alley. We'll show you what you need to do to walk that path with a bounce in your step and, soon, a man at your side.

Oh, the Moves You Will Make …

It all begins with a plan. A written plan is always best, because it's harder to ignore than a plan in your head. This book provides an eight-step plan for taking action toward your goal of a satisfying relationship with a man who provides companionship and/or romance. The plan is based on our experiences and those of friends and acquaintances who have been successful in

A survey distributed by *Family Circle* magazine and whose results were reported by author Gail Sheehy in *New Passages: Mapping Your Life Across Time* found that while life satisfaction dips for women in their late forties, it comes back strong in their fifties, a period of less recorded depression, greater psychological maturity, and even increased psychic abilities.

capturing the hearts of one or more men after age fifty. Each step of the plan suggests actions that you can take to accomplish the step. The women we interviewed for this book shared stories about their progress, sometimes stop-and-go, in forging satisfying relationships. Their voices, along with our own, clearly announced the idea of *movement*, as described below.

Step 1: Box it up; toss it out. Get up and out. The world does not come to you; you have to go get it. Dump the baggage. Ditch the excuses. Build a better you, inside and out. Dye your hair. Buy a few thongs.

Step 2: New people, new places. Shape your own team and your own context. Reconnect with family and friends. Make lifestyle changes: Go back to school or get a new job. Get out of the suburbs!

Step 3: Define and conquer. Figure out your intention. Fun? Flirtation? Occasional companionship? A long-term commitment? Know who the right man is for you so you'll recognize him when you see him.

Step 4: Move into view—his. Cast the net widely, but in the right ocean for your interests. Lose no keepers; keep no losers. Check out all possibilities, new and old. Persist.

Step 5: For fun or forever? A match or a maybe? Use your intuition, your radar, your friends' feedback, and your common sense to determine his fit with your needs. Consider special handling for special cases, including old bachelors, new widowers, and young hunks. Know how to turn his head or capture his heart—whatever part of him you need.

Step 6: On to the good part—better sex now than ever. Prepare the bedroom and the bathroom. Check out the medical issues. Understand his new body and yours. Deal with the libido changes. Grab the lubricant. Be inventive. Be sexy. Enjoy!

Step 7: Step into his arms or into his life. Identify the "real thing." Be in his life, but still have your own life. Deal swiftly and successfully with his kids, your kids, his friends, your friends, his ex, your ex, and other tricky stuff. Get real about finances—his and yours. Become indispensable.

Step 8: Commit to the process. Get a can-do, will-do attitude. Make a plan and put it in writing. Get what you came for!

The steps and corresponding actions we suggest work because they create momentum and energy. When you use this information to write your own plan, using the format in Step 8, it will begin to work for you. Not only will you get out and seek great relationships with men, but by doing so you will become the kind of person that other people want to be with—vigorous, enthusiastic, and fully alive.

The women who will help inspire you as you follow these steps include our gutsy sixty-year-old friend Janis, who moved to Atlanta, Georgia, from Sandusky, Ohio, with a combination of trepidation and hope. She put it this way: "I was reluctant to change, but I had to ask myself if I was living in a social backwater. The answer was a resounding *yes*. Then I had to ask myself why I stayed in that location—especially since, as a nurse, I was professionally mobile. I couldn't find an answer to that one. So, I selected the coast, the better weather, and the explosion of retirees. I plunged into a new life with great energy and a huge lump in my throat. Of course, I was scared of the newness and pretty lonely for a while, but there I was. Within a few months, however, as my fear of the unknown wore off, I realized I also wasn't scared of just about anything else I could think of. After conquering the move, I found it was relatively easy to begin taking up all sorts of new hobbies and friends. Now I have a great social life and terrific male companionship."

Janis may have moved to a better venue for finding mature single men, but her real achievement was to gain personal momentum by discovering that she could claim victory over reluctance to change.

While Janis moved physically, Penny moved in other ways and found that her momentum had a snowball effect. At fifty-eight and living in Washington, D.C., Penny was unhappy about having no committed relationship on the horizon. A visit from an old girlfriend who was a good questioner and a good listener inspired her to examine her patterns. "Although the absence of a committed relationship had been dragging me down for several years, I finally realized that I really didn't care as much about the commitment as about the relationship. I just needed a few fun buddies to join me in some things I like to do. Maybe I'd been giving off scary vibes before, because as soon as I found Don for a golf partner and James to join a ceramics workshop with me, it seemed that more available men just kept coming out of the woodwork."

Penny needed to examine and verbalize her intent before she understood exactly what she wanted. Her eventual discovery of her own desires inspired her to adopt an attitude that was far more likely to bring interesting men into her life.

~~∽

I love men! But I don't need a man.

—SUNNY, 61, UPON MARRYING

HUSBAND NUMBER FOUR

~~∽

We heard success stories again and again from mature women who have been in the dating trenches and now feel fulfilled and accomplished in their relationships with men. We offer their stories as examples and inspiration. We also know that for many readers, inspiration is not enough. We need to nudge women to take the first steps that will start the momentum. Some of you have become comfortable in your nonrelationship mode. Maybe you feel stuck, or, like Emilie, you might tell yourself you're "just not ready yet." We've been there, and it's not a great place. We don't intend to let you linger there past the first chapter of this book. So get ready for a no-nonsense, candid approach that encourages you to take action by adopting the moves that have worked for a lot of women just like you. But, before you start, consider the following checklist:

MADE ANY OF THESE MOVES LATELY?

◇ Gotten a makeover at the best department store cosmetic counter you can find?

◇ Vacationed in a place you've never been before?

◇ Accepted a new job or new responsibilities on the job?

◇ Learned something new and active: Fly tying? Golf? Mountain biking?

◇ Relocated to a new town or new neighborhood?

◇ Upscaled (or even seriously considered upscaling) your car? Your wardrobe? Your health club membership?

◇ Joined a group with a large percentage of men: A martial arts studio? A mixed doubles tennis team? A computer programming class? An investment club?

◇ Showed up at a class reunion? A college alumni trip?

◇ Phoned an old boyfriend?

◇ Reconnected with single girlfriends?

This list, of course, could go on and on. It's about the need for you to get moving and get a life. If you answered *no* to everything on the list, you need to stay up all night and read this book in one sitting. If you answered *no* to most things, you might consider a two- or three-sitting read. If you answered *yes* to most things, you are either a master of the singles scene or a master of exaggeration.

How do you negotiate this unsettling territory? How do you create a more satisfying, joyful life—one with male friends or romances in the picture? We are going to tell you. We've been where you are; so have countless others. We came out of that place with men by our sides. And so will you.

*Discover a
New Attitude and
a New You*

Box It Up; Toss It Out

*M*AYBE YOU RECENTLY BECAME SINGLE. Maybe you recently hit a milestone birthday. What's certain is that you just got another year older. You cannot greet these changes with energy and enthusiasm for what lies ahead—including some terrific relationships with men—if you are mired in the quicksand of baggage, excuses, defenses, delusions, overwork, overmothering or grandmothering, or sheer fright. Fortunately, there are specific actions that can help you shed those attitudes and get ready to move on. Since time is not exactly on your side once you pass the fifty-year mark, start right now.

Your mantra here should be "out with the old." If that sounds a bit harsh, just recall the good feeling you get following a closet-cleaning spree that eliminates jackets with shoulder pads the size of throw pillows and purges a gathered skirt reminiscent of the apron mom wore when washing her victory garden veggies. You will feel even better when you jettison the impediments to enjoying your new stage of adult life.

Getting ready to move requires you to take action in several areas described in this chapter. First, it is important to assess your willingness to confront change. Next, it is time to spend some time on you—both on the outside and inside. What you do in the way of self-improvement will pay off in greater confidence and more energy for embracing a new life. Finally, you need the motivation to leave behind the baggage of your old life and acquire an upbeat attitude about risk, change, and your ability to take small steps that will help move you forward.

Where Are You Now?

Single women past the mid-century mark generally fall somewhere on the following continuum of personal attitudes and actions:

WALLOWING   STRADDLING   REACHING ➤

If you are at the "reaching" stage, you have stored the old baggage and are moving with determination toward new and fulfilling experiences. In that case, you need only some reminders, new perspectives, and support for doing things right. If you are "straddling," you are aware of the advantages of making fresh a start, but wary of the changes required to make it happen. You know you need to let go of parts of your past and move on to your future, and you try in some small ways to do so, but you cannot bring yourself to take the big plunge into the unknown. When you are "wallowing," you are stuck in the past, comfortably clinging to activities, places, and people you became accustomed to years ago but that don't have the same relevance for your current stage of life. If you are wallowing, or even lingering anywhere along the left side of the continuum, you need a serious push toward your new and better life. And, uncomfortable as it may seem, that includes a serious pull away from some elements of your old life.

Candid self-recognition can help. Are you clinging so tightly to old patterns and behaviors that you are unable to allow new patterns to emerge? Even if these new patterns may seem to have no connection to your relationships with men, your ability to embrace them does reflect the openness, interest, and optimism that are necessary to create fulfilling relationships. With that in mind, answer the following questions true or false.

In the past two years:

◇ I have acquired three new people in my life with whom I enjoy spending time.

◇ I have gone back to school to widen my career options or just learn something new.

◇ I have asked for a raise or a new position at work.

◇ I have done something others consider risky. (Sky diving? Contacting a lover from long ago? Challenging the system at work?)

◇ I have done something that announces "me first." (Going to a spa by yourself? Buying yourself a terrific birthday present? Saying no to unreasonable requests at the office? Taking a vacation without your parents, children, or grandchildren?)

◇ I find my reading and television-watching patterns have taken a turn toward more intellectual stimulation.

◇ I have undertaken a major home renovation or redecoration.

◇ I have undertaken a major personal renovation or redecoration. (Weight loss? Face-lift? New hair color?)

◇ I have gotten rid of something large that needed to be pitched or replaced. (An old car? Your adult child's bunk beds?)

If you cannot answer "true" to at least three of these, say hello to your not-so-good buddy Inertia. This little gnome camping out on your shoulder whispers to you a steady stream of excuses for remaining stuck in your rut. If you listen to her words of nonwisdom you might even discover that you have created one of these cozy identities for yourself:

- **The Florence Nightingale:** It's up to you, as a single person who should have plenty of free time, to be chauffeur, nurse, secretary, cook, and errand runner for your parents.

- **The Pin Cushion:** Your children may be grown, but they need to know you will be there to wait on them when they pop back to visit their old homestead in the suburbs.

- **The Violin Player:** You are really too psychologically fragile to deal with a jolt of change right now; maybe in ten years or so. . . .

- **The Sherpa:** You are still loaded down with all the baggage of your past, and you're determined to dwell on it some more before you move on.

- **The Sofa:** Now is your time to sit back, relax, and just see what comes your way.

- **The Groundhog:** It's too risky to get out there and face the world right now. Just stay put until conditions improve.

Where does Inertia come from? *You* invent her, and then you nurture her with notions that simply aren't true. You do this because you are not comfortable with change. You are not convinced that you, at fifty-plus, can leave the moorings of the past and have a fulfilling life as an independent and energetic person. You think that a life lived with as little change and newness as possible is as good as it gets.

In fact, the opposite is true. The women we interviewed who had forged successful romances and friendships with men later in life typically recognized the need for change very early in their experiences as singles past fifty. As Diane, a massage therapist, told us about her life as a newly divorced fifty-four-year-old with adult children out of the nest, "I just knew I had to move on by myself; I couldn't sit and wait for somebody else to make a life for me. I got up, relocated, and got a new job. I was terrified, but what was the point in trying to continue a life that was built around being married and a mom?" The men in her new life weren't far behind.

Give Inertia and her whispered suggestions to you a swift kick out of your life by examining your excuses for staying stuck in your tracks. Notice that these empty excuses are simply the products of fear and self-doubt, and they don't acknowledge the strengths that come from your experience and newfound independence.

You are in the second half of your adult life—the half in which you are more independent, more knowledgeable, more self-aware, more politically and socially savvy, and more professionally competent than ever before. Finally, you are in full flower.

My Next Guy? Not So Fast

But what about the men? Could having one in your life help you get unstuck at this point? Deliberately, we do not entertain

> ### The Full Flower
>
> In the second half of your adult life, you are not the glowing bud of your youth, but you are gloriously in full flower. If you need to be convinced that this means something exciting and sensuous, go to your library and browse art books to view the flower paintings of noted American artist Georgia O'Keeffe. Fully in bloom is fully sexy and fully intriguing. Embrace it; don't waste it.

the idea of a relationship with a man yet. A man is not a life raft you grab to save you from making changes in your life. Instead, you have to build your own life raft. Soon you'll renovate it into a luxury yacht and set it on an appropriate course. Then, and only then, will the men sail over to check it—and you—out. Welcome aboard! But, for now, we'll focus on building that raft and determining how to leave your mooring.

Additionally, a relationship with a man can complicate the serious work of examining and sorting out your life. Dealing with your own life and with a new relationship simultaneously can be like trying to pat your head and rub your tummy at the same time. Don't even attempt it. Let the relationship come along later; then you'll be ready to pat his head while he rubs your tummy.

Katherine still fondly recalls the "guy-atus" she took from men for the first ten months after her divorce. "I was too stressed and gun-shy to think about men, which turned out to be a good thing. I moved to a new house in a new town, took on some new projects at work, volunteered in a political campaign, and helped my two children get off to their freshman year in college. Finally, as I began to feel like an independent and self-confident individual, I was ready to consider male companionship."

I stayed alone and away from everyone for the first three or four months after my husband's death. But I had always wanted to learn about classical music, so I gave myself an intensive course during that time. I bought books and tapes and listened constantly. In a way, I was getting on with my life while grieving, because I was learning. I wasn't really out there, but I wasn't standing still either.

—SARAH, 61, FREELANCE PHOTOGRAPHER

Starting to Change—from the Outside In

At this stage, when you're getting ready to move on, taking steps toward your personal enhancement is often a good place to begin. For example, working on the outer you is a good way to begin building the confidence that can lead to other, seemingly more difficult, changes. We can all get a bit sloppy about our appearance, and we can all look better at any age. This is as true at fifty and older as it was at thirty and younger. How we look is intimately tied to how we feel. And how we feel is linked as tightly as a bicycle chain to how we manage to get up and get going with energy and optimism. So that "superficial" concern about the outer you is a crucial issue for the inner you—and maybe not so superficial after all.

Additionally, by working to improve the outer you, you get the added benefit of focusing your energy and intellect away from unproductive feelings that linger from the past, such as anger, grief, blame, loneliness, helplessness, and low self-esteem. Attending to your appearance is an excellent way to begin the process of moving toward a new and fulfilling life.

There are four areas to consider here:

- Your fitness (firm and healthy)

- Your outer shell (good skin, teeth, hair, nails)

- Your trimmings (clothes and accessories that complement your look)

- Your demeanor (energetic and optimistic)

Where to begin? Here's a tip we discovered from several of our interviewees: Candidly identify your biggest problem from one of the above categories. Maybe you're overweight? Do you have thinning hair? Fankles (fat ankles)? Next, pinpoint your biggest single asset. Great teeth? A pleasing sense of humor? A closet full of Ralph Lauren classics? Begin by selecting one problem and taking steps to solve it. At the same time, select one asset and take steps to emphasize it. Get a haircut and some highlights to give depth to that thinning hair; and, at the same time, invest in a good tooth whitener and practice a bigger smile to show off your teeth. Or, join the nearest gym today and arrange to work out four times a week while you also get those Ralph Lauren skirts and pants altered to the length and fit that allow you to wear them more often.

Hundreds of books, videos, web sites, and other resources are out there to help you with your problem areas, so dedicate some time and energy to determining which diet, which exercise routine, which skin peel, or which fashion look is right for you. To be sure you cover all the bases, check out this list of possibilities:

FOR YOUR FITNESS

◇ Get a baseline health and fitness evaluation: find out about your weight, percentage of body fat, bone density, blood pressure, cholesterol, and cardiovascular health.

◇ Join a gym and use it at least three times a week.

◇ Walk with long, powerful strides everywhere you can.

◇ Use the stairs instead of the elevator whenever you can.

◇ Take up running, bicycling, or other active sports.

◇ Go to yoga, Pilates, or other fitness classes.

◇ Hire a personal trainer.

◇ Determine what changes in eating habits work best for you.

◇ Join a group or club that will support your new diet.

◇ Write down what you eat and calculate the number of calories.

FOR YOUR OUTER SHELL

◇ Get advice from a dermatologist. She can eliminate, minimize, and help prevent many flaws in your skin.

◇ Research, purchase, and use cleansers and moisturizers liberally.

◇ Use a moisturizing cream made especially for the eye area.

◇ Get plenty of sleep.

◇ Have a consultation with a cosmetic surgeon.

◇ Consider peels, abrasions, injections, or surgery.

◇ Consult a vascular surgeon about spider veins and varicose veins.

◇ Find the best possible stylist for a new haircut and color.

◇ Get to the hair salon at least every four to six weeks.

◇ Regularly use a salon for brow waxing, facial hair removal, manicures, and pedicures—or learn how to do these things for yourself well and do them often.

◇ Use a self-tanning gel (better than lotions) when you feel pale.

◇ Use 50 SPF sunblock everywhere and never allow the sun on your unprotected face.

◇ Use a tooth whitener (strips or gels in trays are among the best at-home treatments). If necessary, consult with a cosmetic dentist.

◇ Ditch all your old makeup and start over. If necessary, get help from a makeup specialist or sit for a department store makeover.

～つ

I notice that the women who talk about
"aging gracefully" or about beauty being "skin deep"
are all kind of frumpy looking.

—SEPHINA, 64, AFTER HER SECOND FACE-LIFT

～つ

FOR YOUR TRIMMINGS

◇ Rifle through every closet, every drawer, and every jewelry box: clean them out with the goal of filling several large bags for Goodwill.

- ◇ Restock your leather balm and shoe polish.

- ◇ Get rid of all purses too small or too large.

- ◇ Pay more attention to your shoes; pitch any that appear too worn or too sensible.

- ◇ Get feedback from friends on colors that look best on you.

- ◇ Get feedback from friends on clothes that make you look thinner, younger, sexier, or more professional.

- ◇ Don't go overboard on black, beige, or brown clothes; although they are sometimes the "in" colors, they can also be depressing.

- ◇ Commit to the idea that a few good pieces of jewelry are better than many mediocre ones.

- ◇ Remember that the most important jewelry pieces are those worn near the face and throat—at the eye level of people you meet.

- ◇ Trash the watches that don't work anymore and keep one good one that you can wear on most occasions.

- ◇ Arrange your closet by colors.

- ◇ Put more shelves in your closet. Get the shoes off the floor.

FOR YOUR DEMEANOR

- ◇ Stand up straight; posture counts.

◇ Walk with a bounce.

◇ Smile often (in fact, most of the time).

◇ Be quick to laugh.

◇ Appear open and interested: don't cross your arms.

◇ Listen attentively to anyone speaking to you.

◇ Stop frowning.

◇ Train your eyes wide open, looking ahead, occasionally glancing sideways, and never looking down.

◇ Pick up your energy by drinking fruit juices and eating nutrition bars when necessary.

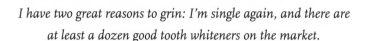

I have two great reasons to grin: I'm single again, and there are at least a dozen good tooth whiteners on the market.

—NANCY, 51, SCHOOL NURSE

For Your Mental Fitness

We all know that interesting women are attractive at any age—to their friends, to their families . . . and to men. These are the ladies who are aware of what is happening in the world, interested in a wide range of issues and ideas, and enthusiastic about new opportunities to learn and experience. They can reel off a half dozen animals on the endangered species list and discuss the pros and cons of trillion-dollar federal deficits. You can only get that way by exercising your mind—reading, listening, reflecting, conversing, and learning in areas that allow you to stretch and grow.

Take stock of what you do now that might or might not exercise your mind. Are the last three books you read a cookbook, a needlework book, and a romance novel? Do your magazine subscriptions heavily favor home decorating and Hollywood gossip? What do you watch on television? (Please don't say home shopping!) What do you listen to on the radio? You may need some serious intellectual stimulation—the kind that will challenge your mental faculties and make you a more interesting person. Even if you already do some things that exercise your mind, you can always do more. Like work on the outer you, work on the inner you never ends. Consider your intellectual workout from two perspectives: the communication you soak in (it's all around you; just tune in) and the communication you seek out (delve into new situations with interest and curiosity).

The good news is that undertaking improvement in these areas requires very little additional time or money. The idea is simply to make changes to the activities that you are probably already doing in order to make them more intellectually stimulating and to make you a more interesting and more fulfilled person. The following lists offer some ways to get started.

The Communication You Soak In

◇ Watch more television news; vary your fare to include *C-SPAN* and weekly news review programs such as *This Week* and *Meet the Press.*

◇ Regularly check out news on the Internet, as well as chat rooms about newsworthy topics. Consider an electronic subscription to a newspaper that you wouldn't otherwise receive.

◇ View instructional television programs, like those on the History Channel or the National Geographic Explorer series. Documentary programs and miniseries, such as those on PBS, are both illuminating and entertaining.

◇ Listen to informative radio programming, like National Public Radio, as much as possible, especially if you commute to work in your car.

◇ Expand your musical horizons to include unfamiliar styles—jazz, blues, rap, classical, country, or other genres. You can discover new interests on the radio and then pursue them further through a library that lends CDs or by purchasing CD anthologies.

◇ Don't stop at your local newspaper; at least once or twice a week, read a good national newspaper such as the *New York Times, Washington Post,* or *USA Today.*

◇ Always have a good book handy on your nightstand. Include biographies, histories, essay collections, and Pulitzer Prize winners in your reading.

◇ Expand your magazine reading to include more highbrow publications like *The New Yorker, Atlantic Monthly, Saturday Review,* and others.

THE COMMUNICATION YOU SEEK OUT

◇ Check out programming at bookstores and public libraries in your area to find book readings and signings, lecture series, and book groups. Attend these, or simply browse the library and bookstore shelves for new books from time to time.

◇ Join a book club and attend regularly. You might want to start your own group or ask acquaintances about existing groups. Inquire at libraries and bookstores about clubs that meet on their premises. Check out SeniorNet.org, an organization that supports shared knowledge among computer users over fifty, and consider joining its online book discussion group. The Great Books Foundation, emphasizing classic literature, sponsors scores of local book clubs that meet regularly in nearly every state. The contact information for these groups is available at GreatBooks.org.

◇ Join groups that sponsor discussions about current events, like the League of Women Voters or a local business roundtable. National groups with local chapters generally post contact information about those chapters on their web sites.

◇ Attend museum and gallery openings.

◇ Be in the front row at lectures at your local college.

◇ Attend educational seminars sponsored by local nonprofit groups on everything from financial planning to consumer law. Contact your local chamber of commerce or visitors bureau for a monthly calendar of such events, check weekly newspapers, and consult the event calendars of colleges and school districts in your area.

◇ Attend the symphony, the opera, and other performances.

◇ Include in your video and film viewing some documentaries and limited-release independent films, often screened at art-house movie theaters.

Travel Tales for the Guy Back Home

Carol, widowed and left with an empty nest at fifty-five, decided to pursue educational travel by joining the alumni trips offered through her alma mater. She raised the neces-

sary cash by selling her husband's high-end Mercedes and buying a used Toyota Camry for less than half of her profit. After her first trip, which included summer seminars at Oxford University, she was hooked. "The history and literature we learned about were fascinating," she recalled. "I was suddenly ready to soak up every factoid I'd avoided in college history courses, and I felt like a real scholar for being back in the learning seat."

Later, Carol learned about Incan and Mayan art in Mexico and about environmentally sound land management in Australia. Unexpectedly, her Australia experiences came into play when she spoke to the owner of a new wine bar in her town about Australian vintages. He was so impressed by her knowledge that he asked her to run an Australian wine tasting evening; later, he was so impressed by her curiosity and intelligence that he asked her out to dinner. They have now been dating for three years.

Carol never met any single men she was interested in romancing on the alumni educational trips. However, she clearly became a more knowledgeable, curious, and interesting woman through her experiences. She also became more self-assured through her newfound capacity for intellectual stimulation. When a potential romantic partner did cross her path, she was ready for him.

Attitude Adjustment

Although your attitude is an elusive and highly personal quality that reflects your inner spirit, your beliefs, and your sense of well-being, it is not invisible to the rest of the world. Think of the women you know who have positive attitudes. They are optimistic, energized, creative, and fun to be around. They worry little and whine infrequently. They are bustling with new and interesting projects and plans. They don't dwell on problems or let small setbacks stop their forward movement. The women with negative attitudes are a very different story, and we don't even want to go there.

Clearly, a positive attitude is important in order to fully enjoy life, much less attract men who can enjoy it in your company; and even if your attitude is pretty good, it can always stand to get better. Fortunately, adjusting your attitude for the better is not as difficult as it sounds. The key is to *do* things *as if* your attitude were already there. Commit, persist, and don't slip back into any negative patterns. Here are some examples of activities that can support your attitude adjustment:

◇ Make a pact with a friend to cheer each other up and take each other out as soon as the whining and negativity start for either one of you.

◇ Keep a journal. Write about your actions and feelings in it on days you feel positive. Reread it from time to time to discover patterns that link actions to attitudes.

◇ When one part of your life is dragging you down (maybe your work seems endlessly routine), reflect on it only very briefly. Then, do something new and energizing in another part of your life (perhaps acquire a pet or plan a visit to a fun friend in another state) until you are ready to approach your problem with a sense of certainty that you can solve it.

◇ Don't dwell on problems. Do not dramatize your need for minor surgery by talking about it incessantly. In fact, try to mention it only when absolutely necessary. Then get it done and get over it. Don't dwell on the savings you should have but don't. Consult a financial advisor, establish a solid plan for the future, and spend as little time as possible worrying about monthly statements.

◇ When things go wrong (car problems, expensive home repairs, lost luggage), limit your fuming and fretting to no more than a day. After that, simply take action and get over it.

◇ Take stock of someone you know who has a positive attitude and notice her physical presence—her posture, body language, stride, and smile. When you feel negative, imitate that positive look.

◇ Think of a friend who has a way of always making you feel good without letting you wallow in your problems. Get in touch with that friend whenever you need a jolt of positive attitude.

◇ When you feel sorry for yourself, go for a power walk or a run. When you feel unloved, visit the zoo. When you have the winter blahs, buy something new to wear in melon or canary yellow. When you feel like crying, rent a silly comedy on DVD. When you make a mistake, respond with a giggle and "Oh my gosh, I must be daffy" (not a frown and "I'm so stupid, I can't do anything right"). When you feel you've been wronged, break out your favorite upbeat music and dance around your home with a smile on your face. When you feel like nothing works, seek counsel through a church or community spiritual group.

At this point, the idea is not necessarily to *meet* somebody, but to *be* somebody. Dumb blondes and helpless Harriets are only attractive as teenagers or as hood ornaments. At our age a woman who is fascinating inside and out will get a lot farther.

Building Momentum

Once you've spent some time attending to your personal enhancement inside and out, you're ready to think about more major changes. These changes can be achieved either in baby steps or in one big plunge. The big plunge is a serious life change, like a new job or a move to another town. It rarely happens immediately after becoming single or being single and confronting a milestone birthday. More likely, it happens after months, or even years, of reflection and baby steps.

One Brief Trip Leads to One Big Relocation

We were amazed when our friend Deena decided on both a new job and a new location only a year after she sent her philandering husband packing. She had lived all but seven of her fifty-one years in Des Moines, Iowa; her parents, sister, and brother all lived within a three-hour drive; and her two grown sons still lived only minutes from her home. As a surgical prep nurse who occasionally taught at the nearby community college, Deena had a network of professional contacts that eventually led to a lucrative job offer as the Chicago regional sales manager for a surgical instrument manufacturer. When we mentioned our surprise that she decided to accept the offer and move hundreds of miles away, Deena reminded us, "Well, in that first year after my divorce, I took two two-week trips to Mexico to work in those remote missionary clinics. That really gave me a different perspective on people, on the reality of poverty, and on the smallness of my little world. I was with amazing medical colleagues from all over the country, and I guess I realized there are good people everywhere out there. Being in a new place doesn't change that."

The first steps you take, although small, can be the most important. Here are some steps that women we interviewed described as giving them momentum for later leaps. Read them to get ideas and then add your own.

SMALL STEPS FOR GIVING

◇ Perform service through a church mission (build homes in foreign countries, read to inner-city preschool students, cut back underbrush at a charity summer camp).

◇ Volunteer at an animal shelter (transport hopeful adoptee dogs and cats to a mall on weekends, clean cages, restock food and water).

◇ Volunteer at a food bank (shelve cans, take inventory, pick up donations).

◇ Tutor in an after-school program (help with homework, teach computer skills, assist in library searches).

◇ Take a volunteer vacation (ask your travel agent).

◇ Serve on a community board (such as for the library, the symphony, or public parks and recreation).

SMALL STEPS FOR YOU

◇ Learn a new sport (take kayaking lessons, attend a golf clinic, get racquetball instruction).

◇ Attend "how to" classes in just about anything (find them through your local home and hardware center, sports store, or college continuing education division).

◇ Join a bicycling group for weekend rides (the bike shops in your area will have a calendar of events).

◇ Join a group (an investment club, a yoga studio, a writers' circle).

◇ Sign up for on-the-job training in new technologies at your workplace.

◇ Participate in an acting workshop (through your community theater or local college theater department).

Think of It as Getting a Chance, Not Taking a Chance

The big plunge—a life change that results in a new home, a new location, a new job, or relationships with new people—seems so risky. Even considering a major change may give you the disorienting feeling of a rug being pulled out from under you. What rug? The rug that cushions the rut you are standing in? The rug that makes you more comfortable standing still on the floor than leaping for the sky? In fact, pulling that old rug out from under you is a very good thing. Although it may cause some temporary discomfort, it will also lead to long-term benefits and will inspire amazed reactions, peppered with hints of envy, from your friends.

I was a single woman bored with the same old,
same old me. I just wanted change, and I had some savings.
So I moved to a lovely and funky mountain town in Idaho,
where I knew not one person. After I slowly made a new and
better personal and professional life, old friends told me,
"I wish I had your courage; I'd be way too scared to do
something like that." I always reply, "I was way too
scared to not do something like that."

—ELLEN, 66, LIBRARIAN

Financial issues—those involving both long-term financial security and short-term up-front costs—comprise the largest group of excuses given to us by women who cannot bring themselves to move away from their old lives. Interestingly, most of the women who use these excuses have significant resources, such as job skills and experience that are readily transferable to other locations and other professions, homes that can be sold for enough money to buy the next home, savings accounts and insurance policies that can be tapped for the security deposit at the next apartment, and cars that are paid off. If these resources aren't available to you, start saving *now.* Take a second job, if necessary; it's that important. In a year or two, you will be able to step out of your rut. One caution: Don't even think about touching your retirement savings.

> **Risk and Be Smart**
>
> Bill Treasurer, author of *Right Risk: Ten Powerful Principles for Taking Giant Leaps with Your Life,* advises that smart risks are the ones that match our principles and values. No matter what the outcome, those risks are valuable for helping us achieve the development and self-affirmation that cannot happen if we are overcome by worries about our safety.

The second most common excuse for remaining in the old, familiar rut is the fear of risk. Many women we interviewed were reluctant to experience the discomfort that comes when faced with the uncertainty of change. Yet there are some new things you actually *want* to do that have uncertain outcomes, like committing to a man you think you love. So maybe you are not as determined to avoid risk as you think. You might simply be selective about the risks you take. In that case, you need to reflect and examine why that is.

If you want to plunge in and make a significant change, but seem to always butt up against the "too risky" excuse, reflect and gather courage by asking yourself:

> ❧ What meaning does this "risky" change have for me? Does it speak to some of my core values, like increasing my

independence, satisfying my curiosity, continually learning, or taking on new professional challenges?

🦋 What will a day in my life be like one year from now if I take the risk and make the big change? What will it be like if I stay put?

🦋 What are the likely by-products of making this change (increased self-confidence, personal growth)? What are the likely by-products of staying put?

🦋 Does my reluctance to make a change speak to what I think and value, or does it reflect the standards of others?

🦋 Are there any baby steps I can take that will increase my passion for making a big change and improve my chances for success?

🦋 What are the three most important reasons for my reluctance to make the change I am considering? Are any *really* impossible to confront? Exactly what steps, and according to what timetable, can I take to address them?

🦋 If I make a big change, what's the worst that can happen? The best?

🦋 Ten years from now, will I regret the risks not taken?

🦋 Is there someone I can talk to about this potential change who can offer support, ideas, and enthusiasm?

A third excuse for avoiding change noted by many women is their families. Transformations that might alter relationships with or distance from parents, children, or grandchildren provoke all manner of excuses for inertia. You can't take the promotion that will entail a lot of travel because you need to be available to baby-sit the grandchildren. You can't move thirty miles away to that more cosmopolitan community because you would no longer be within a block of the aging parents whom you check on nearly every day.

Many a lifelong spinster has been victim to "they need me" syndrome. Family members particularly seem to need you when you are single, female, and past midlife. They rarely need their younger, male, or married relatives. What does that tell you about the authenticity of their need? Do they really *need* you? Do they even *want* to be dependent on you? How much of their neediness is about your interpretation of their needs or your subconscious desire to be needed? Clearly, if the "they need me" syndrome is a source of immobility for you, it is time to examine the reality of this need and where it comes from. This excuse for staying in your rut is the saddest of all, because it is often based on erroneous assumptions, and because there are many ways for your family's needs to be filled that do not require *you* to become a fossil.

The final source of women's excuses for an inability to make a major change is lack of self-confidence. This old familiar problem results in statements like "I'd never be able to accomplish that" or "That would never work out for me."

This can't-do thinking creates a fear of failure that stops you dead in your tracks. It happens when you have not given yourself permission to be imperfect, to make mistakes, to embrace the idea of learning from things that go wrong. Katherine once worked in an organization whose top people did a lot of public speaking. She was about to turn down an offer of a promotion to that group when one of them admitted to her, "I feel so much better in my work now that I've given myself permission to bomb every once in a while." With that understanding, Katherine accepted the promotion and began a great deal of public speaking. She did bomb once in a while, but so what? She had permission.

You are not perfect, and you will make mistakes. But if you give yourself permission to be flawed and to take a wrong turn now and then, you will not let worries about these realities stop you from making the changes you need to make.

Parting Thoughts

In the final analysis, only you can shape a more fulfilling life. In this chapter we have suggested actions and offered support for becoming a better you, inside and out. Finding the motivation to continue requires you to understand that change is a positive force that renews and energizes and is usually a whole lot less risky than making no changes at all. You can start the ball rolling today if you get up, get out, and get a new you.

Build a Great Team
and Choose a Good
Location

NEW PEOPLE, NEW PLACES

*C*HANGE IS ON THE WAY. It starts with a decision to venture out with vitality into a world of new people, places, and actions, to confront with energy and optimism the context in which you live your life. While the previous chapter addressed the necessity of making changes to *you*—improving your look, your mind, and your attitude—we are now suggesting that you do something about the world around you. That world includes your family and friends, your work, your personal interests, and your home. Makeovers in these areas are, ultimately, do-overs—chances to make a fresh start.

Even though many of the faces and places in your life will stay the same, the way you encounter them when you are single and fifty-plus may be very different than when you were younger or part of a couple. Your stepfather's son-in-law,

Tim—whom you always secretly referred to as "Dim"—turns out to be a fun and witty companion for a night on the town after a family reunion. You reshuffle the time spent with your five best female friends in favor of never-married Bonnie and widowed Susan, who both offer to help you tune up your mountain bike; the other three are busy planning their daughters' baby showers and decorating their retirement condominiums in Florida. Your gay next-door neighbors, one a hospital orderly and one a security guard, seem more interesting over a glass of wine after work than the colleagues at your corporate office. These are not necessarily the relationships you expected.

In other words, your world is already changing. If you have been resisting that change, you have been resisting moving toward the life that will eventually include fulfilling relationships with men. However, if you embrace your new situation, you can use it strategically to help move toward the life and the relationships you seek. Don't cheat yourself by avoiding new encounters or attempting to cling to your old context. This is the time for significant rejuvenation, including renewed and new relationships with family and friends toward building an effective network of support and assistance, as well as changes in your location, profession, or personal interests that will help you develop a new and fulfilling life.

Family: Ties That Bind, but Not Too Tightly

Ask any ten people about their fondest thought as they gaze on a sea of family members around a large Thanksgiving table, and, if they were honest, at least one would say, "I'm fondly thinking that tomorrow someone will tell me I was adopted." The other nine, however, would describe the good feelings that come from enduring family bonds that might be reconfigured but are never broken. Relationships with family, both immediate and extended, change as various members move far away, become busy with their own immediate families, move back into town, age, find new common ground, and pass away. But, in general, by the second half of your adult life, you've moved in the direction of a stronger sense of attachment to your family.

In our own experience we have usually been physically distant from our families. After decamping for college, neither of us ever again lived in the same state as our parents. After graduation, we never lived in the same state with each other. Our many cousins, aunts, and uncles also scattered far from us. Yet, as we reached our middle years, we got back in touch. Cousin Robert visited Katherine and her family in Utah and even lived at her house for several months. Cousin Cassie visited Emilie and her family in Chicago. During visits to our parents in Florida, we contacted a number of cousins who lived nearby. As our aunts, uncles, and parents became older, and especially as they became terminally ill, both of us become closer with all of our cousins and their spouses. By the time Emilie was widowed and Katherine was divorced, we had discovered a family full of people who related in new ways and were ready sources of support.

When you're fifty-plus and single, it's a great time to get reacquainted with family, which is an excellent way to move toward embracing your new life. Admittedly, some family members will remind you why you lost touch in the first place. However, if you have not spent a lot of time with some relatives in recent years, you might be surprised at some changes for the better. You'll probably discover that common experiences abound: "You're not the only sap; I had Enron stock when it tanked too." Or "Same thing happened to me: I quit hormone replacements after the findings about cancer, but crawled back to the doctor and begged on hands and knees for them after the fifth hot flash." "I guess we're not a family of geniuses; I also never once filled out the federal loan forms correctly while my kids were in college."

Genetic ties, a common family history, and similar experiences are the basis for getting exactly what you need at this time in your life:

- ❧ Caring support about the changes you are confronting

- ❧ A kick in the butt to encourage you to take charge of the changes you are confronting

❧ Introductions to others, including men, who can help you deal with the changes you are confronting

～

I barely knew my 56-year-old cousin and his girlfriend, but they lived near my mother and hosted me on weekend visits after she broke her hip. They turned out to be fun-loving, upbeat people who often dragged me to their favorite piano bar, which we closed many Saturday nights and where I began meeting people for the first time since my messy divorce. Later, I wrote a country song, "Nursing Home Days, Piano Bar Nights."

—CAROLINE, 59, PIANO TEACHER

～

ALL IN THE FAMILY: LET THEM BE FRIENDS

Even if some of your family members seem nothing like you in lifestyle and demeanor, they can still have your best interests at heart. Consider the following scenario: You, a sixty-year-old widow of two years, are visiting back in Garden City, where family is gathered for the funeral of the family's ninety-three-year-old matriarch, your Auntie Millie. There have been much eating and drinking, many exchanges of stories and photos, and much laughter and tears as your twenty-six relatives who have not seen each other in a long time get reacquainted. Over a family brunch, you chat with your cousin Mel, the once pimply kid who is a silver fox at age sixty-five, and his fourth wife, Lou, a flashy and overbearing forty-nine-year-old who prompted your catty cousin Jessica to whisper to you, "Look who's stalking."

"You come visit us sometime, you hear," says Mel.

You: "That would be so difficult. My schedule . . ."

Lou: "Well, we're right smack in the middle of West Palm Beach. It's a happening place and only about a six-hour drive from you in Brunswick. We'll just adopt you and coddle you the whole time. We've got a big ol' guest bedroom suite. I decorated it myself."

You: "It's always so hard to get away from my work."

Mel: "Here's the schedule: Early morning surf casting for blues; a short jog down to the pier for orange juice and biscuits; swimming and reading time by the pool at home; lunch al fresco at one of our oceanfront restaurants. We'll do a barbecue dinner at our place so you can meet a few of the good buddies I told you about—some single. Then maybe some swanky barhopping."

You: "Maybe next year, after things calm down at the office . . ."

Wait! What is not to like about this offer? Sure, these people aren't your best friends, but they are caring relatives who will get you up and out and might even introduce you to some interesting men. They are offering to help you get into position, sample what is out there, and have some time away. And they really do live in a happening location. A better response would have been "I'd love to come, and I've wanted to get away next month. But, after the way I've been run around at work, I need lots of time to relax and do nothing. So promise me you won't be put off if I bring a good book and spend some time buried in it by the pool."

ALL IN THE FAMILY: VALUE THE IMPACT

Your family, who usually know you from way back when and understand you better than anyone, can also help you get to know your strengths and weaknesses. Consider the following scenario: You are on a business trip to the city where your divorced cousin Sarah and her married brother Dan both live. Their mother, your still-vigorous eighty-two-year-old Aunt Mary, has just moved to an assisted living apartment nearby. You plan a reunion evening with the three of them, which begins at a French restaurant and continues at an Irish pub after you take Aunt Mary back to her apartment. You are all a little bit tipsy and somewhat loose-tongued when you begin to reminisce about the past.

> *You:* Sarah, you made me cringe when we were kids. Little Miss Perfect. Remember how every Thanksgiving you'd make tiny cardboard place cards for everyone, and you always recited a long and well-rehearsed Thanksgiving prayer?

Sarah: I really was hard to take, but I was intimidated by your ability to join the boys in everything from poker games to touch football. And what a mouthy little thing you could be.

Dan: Right—mouthy and extremely loud. Some of those poker games were excruciating.

You: Oh, thanks lots. Like, Dan, you were so perfect—big ears and bad breath.

Sarah (giggling): How much has really changed?

Dan (giggling): Lots. Like, I hardly ever punch you in the arm like I used to.

You: And we all drink quite a bit more.

Sarah (more serious): And you are really a different person in so many ways.

You: Ugh; everyone changes. Let's not even go there.

Wait! You just ignored a golden opportunity for some candid feedback about you from some of the people who know you best and care about you pretty much unconditionally. Accurate feedback is invaluable information that can help you determine what you need to work on about yourself. It's very difficult to obtain from anyone except family, or from anyone whose tongue hasn't been loosened a bit for one reason or another. You've got both here, so don't miss the opportunity. A better response:

You: "You're right about that, Sarah. So, okay, tell me what you think is most different about me—good and bad. I really need the feedback, and from you too, Dan. I honestly have no idea how I appear to others, and I would love to hear about it. And I promise not to get defensive. Tell me everything. If you want, I'll even reciprocate. Heck, we're family."

This Team's for You

Think of your family as your team—a team that you might need to build by reestablishing communication with some members you haven't seen in years. Your team of family members is more than simply a network of contacts. Even dysfunctional families will often eventually come around and manage to encourage and support you in amazing ways. And although family members may not direct you to new men, new career opportunities, or new interests outside work immediately when you enlist their support, they won't forget you once they know you are looking. Six months later you will get a call from your brother suggesting you take a look at a new accounting position that just opened in the Dallas branch of his financial services company. Your sister will call and say, "Definitely stop by here the next time you take a trip to San Francisco. My friend Gerald is dying to meet you." And, of course, Cousin Mel with the gold chain around his neck will always label his emails with the subject line "Come on Down."

The following are some important guidelines for building your family team:

- **Get in touch:** Contact family members you rarely see, including some distant relatives you can't recall ever meeting, and get to know them.

- **Learn:** Aunt Elna haunts flea markets and knows a lot about antiques. Cousin Sam is a whiz at swing dancing. Let them educate you. Learning about their hobbies is interesting, and it may come in handy later.

- **Open up:** Admit that you want to get moving but need some help.

- **Be explicit:** Let them know you are open to a new job, a new location, new interests and activities, and especially new men.

- **Be more explicit:** Ask for their assistance. ("Let me know if you hear about any new opportunities in my field of work." "Let me know if you stumble across any men who might be a fit for me." "Let me know if you hear of anything that might interest me in the way of travel, volunteer work, or learning opportunities.")

- **Remember:** The urge to be in touch with relatives increases as we reach middle age and beyond. Your family members—even distant or long-silent ones—really do want to hear from you and see you. Furthermore, you probably have some cousins, aunts, uncles, or other relatives who would love to take a mini-vacation and come visit you. Invite them. Occasionally host the Thanksgiving dinner at your house and volunteer your support and assistance when relatives need help.

Friends: In Need, in Deed . . . and Not

As members of the team that provides support, ideas, and motivation to help you get moving, friends may sometimes be more effective than relatives. After all, you get to pick your friends. And at various times you unpick them by staying in touch only through Christmas cards or by losing touch altogether. There's nothing wrong with a little weeding out from time to time as the friendship fit fades.

A Friendly Match for Mismatched Friends

Lizbeth, living in Richmond, Virginia, had eleven tennis teammates whom she counted as good friends when she divorced at age fifty-three. Not surprisingly, during the year of her separation she became closest to teammate Elaine, who had filed for a divorce only six months earlier. Lizbeth, originally from Maine and a corporate attorney with a closet full of black business suits, and Elaine, a tank-topped landscape architect from Alabama, seemed like the quintessential odd couple. However, they joined together to figure out how

---

to approach post-divorce family holidays, to help each other pack up and move to new locations, and to laugh about their first attempts at dating as divorcées. They also took several weekend trips together to get away and relax. As Lizbeth explained, "Elaine became an important lifeline to me, and I was the same for her. We each needed a buddy who was high on understanding and instantly available for assistance. A year or two later, we both started looking to friends who understood not only our divorces, but also our work and our past experiences; but that friendship has been invaluable and will last a lifetime."

Just as some friendships start or are strengthened as your marital status changes or as you become older, others seem to fade. You might notice that your life as a newly single person is no longer in sync with those of your married friends. But don't assume anything. Some of your married friends will continue to be solid members of your support team because you still have a lot in common: you might be employed by the same company, attend a pottery workshop together, or live next door to one another. Other friends, both male and female, will start spending more time with their other buddies.

When a friendship starts to fade, recognize its twilight stage quickly and move on. A friend who was once a tight pal may withdraw his or her attention or spend less time doing things

> *Cosmopolitan* magazine matriarch Helen Gurley Brown
> said it more than twenty years ago in her book *Having
> It All,* and it is still true: "God forbid there should not be
> romantic love in your life, but even worse might be the
> world without the archangels who are 'only' your friends."

with you. You may never know why. For now, however, simply assume there have been changes in your interests. You may very well become close again at a later date, but right now concentrate on positive friendships that can help you move forward.

It is important to distinguish positive from negative friendships very quickly and lose the negative ones without wasting time—like deleting unwanted email before you even open it. Positive friendships are those that leave you feeling supported and optimistic about your movement toward a new and fulfilling life. Negative friendships are those that waste your time and leave you worried and uncertain about your ability to move forward. You'll recognize the types.

Examples of positive friends are:

- **Hal the Helper:** He comes over to look under the hood when you tell him your car is making a funny noise. When he can't figure it out, he calls *Car Talk* for you.

- ❦ **Sharon the Shoulder:** She empathizes with you and supports you by encouraging you to talk about your problems and providing lots of chicken soup, a great cabernet, and chocolate cheesecake.

- ❦ **Erika the Energizer:** She will not let you wallow. Don't try to tell her you feel a cold coming on; there's a new upscale sports bar in town, and for the gala opening she has reserved a table for a group of eight, and one seat has your name on it.

- ❦ **Ronald the Realist:** He plays upbeat bullshit detector when you tell him your veterinarian seems flirty. "Oh, come on! A 55-year-old bachelor? I don't think so! You can do way better."

Examples of negative friends are:

- ❦ **Morley the Mole:** He could easily drag you down with him as he pleads too tired to go to a movie, too disinterested to go to a restaurant, and too bored to attend a museum opening.

- ❦ **Spencer the Sponge:** Her goal is to soak up your support without offering any of her own. "Let's stop at the hospital so you can visit with my mom. Then we'll go out to dinner and discuss how we'll do the food for that baby shower I'm giving my niece."

- **Shelly the Shredder:** She has decided that all men are worthless. "How can you stand working with Paul? He's even more clueless than those three losers in technical support put together. We definitely don't need these people."

- **Inga the Insensitive:** She forgets to include you in plans that involve everyone else on the block, and your phone calls go unreturned.

It is almost impossible to turn negative friends into positive ones without investing more time and energy than it is worth. If you confront them, they will likely become defensive; and if you don't, you'll be kicking yourself around the block. Your only alternative is to ignore them for now by pleading too busy. Let them reinvent themselves and reenter your orbit at a later date. On the other hand, positive friends need to be nurtured and encouraged or they might soon feel unappreciated. Accept their contributions eagerly and graciously.

Friendly Persuasion: View Candor as Caring

A year ago you reconnected with James, whom you knew in high school and who recently moved back to your hometown. You both understand that there is no romantic potential here, but you enjoy occasional friendly lunches and afternoon bike rides. You laugh easily together and feel comfortable acting silly and airing outrageous thoughts.

James: "The way you got that hostess to move us to a different table was masterful—reminded me of the old Greenview High School stuck up girls all over again."

You: "What do you mean 'stuck up'?"

James: "Oh, that was a bad choice of words. I guess I just mean that you and your high school girlfriends used to intimidate me with your collective self-assured assertiveness, and that hasn't changed."

You: "You're telling me I'm something like arrogant?"

James: "Not really. Just a touch more sure of yourself than a lot of men might be able to handle. Let's face it, you have reason to be; you're smart and beautiful. But an awful lot of us still want to see a woman's vulnerable side."

You: "An awful lot of you seem to interpret 'self-assurance' as 'arrogance' when it shows up in a woman. But you don't interpret it so negatively when it shows up in a man."

Wait! You are getting way too defensive. This is a caring friend who is telling you something you need to know about yourself and your possible effect on men. He's not trying to hurt or anger you. Consider it a goodwill gesture when a friend takes the time to reveal something personal about you. Encourage it with something like "You guys can be such sissies, but I guess I have to deal with that. So, what, exactly, do I have to do to be seen as somewhat vulnerable and not excessively self-assured?"

Friendly Persuasion: Enjoy Each Act of Kindness

You've had a rough day—the weather is cold and rainy, and it's the third year anniversary of your husband's death. When you get home from work, you feel tired and glum. Just after you pull on a pair of sweats, the phone rings. It's Marla, a fellow widow and a friend of the past two years.

Marla: "I know this is a very rough day for you, so I thought I'd drop by with some Chinese takeout."

You: "Oh, I couldn't eat a thing."

Marla: "Well, you could try; and we'll just stash it in the fridge if you still have no appetite."

You: "If you insist."

An hour later, Marla arrives.

Marla: "I picked up a small gift for you: that Etta James CD you love. Let's put it on."

You: "I'll listen to it later. I'm not in the mood now."

Marla: "Look, I've been there; I am there. We can talk."

You: "Maybe another time."

Wait! Don't push away a friend who has the experience and understanding to be empathetic. You will badly need her on your team if you want to be able to move ahead toward

Research by Shelley E. Taylor, a professor of psychology at UCLA, found that women seek out friendships, especially during stressful times, as part of their nurturing instinct. Her book *The Tending Instinct: Women, Men, and the Biology of Our Relationships* notes that social support provided by friendships decreases blood pressure and allows women to cope with stress, which possibly explains why women outlive men.

more fulfilling times. She will eventually drift away if you continue to make her feel unwelcome. Even when you are tired and sad, try to respond to positive friends gracefully:

> *You:* "I'm pretty down, so you might have to carry the conversation, but I'm really glad you're here."

Always remember that you need a team, a network of people who can introduce you to new opportunities, new people, and new places. Friends join family members in enlarging your network and improving your chances to establish fulfilling personal and romantic relationships. But your friends and family can't help you if you don't let them. Encourage them; let them know what you need; ask them for support and ideas; take their feedback seriously, and reciprocate by being a good friend to them.

Lifestyle Makeovers: Extreme and Otherwise

In Step 1, we asked you to examine your attitude toward risk and change, and we suggested that you consider the barriers holding you back and the baby steps that can ready you for a big plunge. Now it is time to confront that plunge and make a change to your lifestyle. This might take the form of moving to a new location, changing your profession, or developing a new personal interest. By changing your lifestyle you open new doors to new people, actions, and places. Is it necessary? Not if you want nothing in your life to change. But if you want nothing to change, why are you reading this book?

Ultimately, you want to develop a fulfilling relationship—either a romantic relationship or a friendship—with a man or men. And your chances of that happening are much worse if you continue to live your life pretty much the same way you have been than if you make some major changes. To be clear, adopting a stray kitten is not a major change. Neither is repainting your kitchen or traveling to one more professional conference this year than last. A big change is being elected to city council, moving downtown from the suburbs, taking a new job, writing a book, or taking up marathon running. These are the sorts of changes that will spill over into many aspects of your life and keep doing so for a number of years.

Job Moves: Up or Elsewhere

Since we know so few women who adore their jobs so much that they wouldn't consider leaving them, let's start here. (If you happen to be one of the lucky few who dearly loves her job, skip this part, but only after you subject yourself to our crucial question, "Oh *really?*") For the rest of you, the question of the moment is "Why are you there if you aren't happy with your job?"

You might think you are too close to retirement to "lose" your pension. The reality is that you may not lose anything by leaving your job prior to retirement age, taking your vested retirement savings, and getting into a new, possibly better, plan for five or ten years. Investigate your situation by talking to a financial planner who can read the fine print on your retirement plan's policy statements. Unless you are a public employee in a state that has an anti-retirement incentive plan, such as increased pay for staying X years beyond retirement age, there may be little or no advantage in retirement benefits for hanging onto employment that makes you stressed or unhappy.

You might also believe that nobody will hire a woman beyond fifty, or perhaps even forty. A man, maybe; a woman, never. Yes, age discrimination is real, but it doesn't happen in every circumstance. You can easily make the case that you have plenty of job experience, and hopefully you have continually developed necessary skills to keep pace with new job requirements. By now you are hopefully an expert at identifying whether a job is a good fit, and you are unlikely to leave a position quickly because you suddenly discovered it wasn't the job for you. For most employers, hiring an older worker who is willing to stay five or ten years is a better investment than churning through younger workers every two years. And finally, we do know many women who have managed successfully to avoid indicating their ages on resumes and applications.

Perhaps you have decided that even though your work doesn't thrill you, it provides a decent paycheck for doing things you are accustomed to without the stress of learning new systems, confronting new people, and proving yourself all over again. That's fair. But be sure, then, that you are taking advantage of the ease that your current work provides—long weekends, long lunch hours, time to pursue with passion new hobbies and sports, opportunities to learn, opportunities to volunteer, opportunities to moonlight. If your job doesn't thrill you but you are committed to staying, make it as small a part of your life as possible and spend leftover time and energy on other parts of your life.

If you do decide to change jobs, remain flexible and consider all your options. Relocation to a new organization is only one possibility. You may be able to find a stimulating new position—either a promotion or a lateral move—within your current organization, or you may be able to take on new duties and responsibilities in your current job.

According to career development consultant Beverly L. Kaye, author of *Up Is Not the Only Way: A Guide to Developing Workforce Talent*, "There is no single way for a person to move." She suggests that employees looking for professional change consider lateral moves and even downward moves within their organizations as first steps toward achieving longer-term goals.

Life Outside Employment

If you spend forty or fifty hours a week gainfully employed, that leaves more than twice as many hours to do other things, including sleep. You can change your life substantially by making significant changes in how you spend your waking hours when not at work.

From Postdivorce Pastime to Full-Time Job

Janet, divorced at fifty-eight and living in the Chicago suburbs, was working part-time at a flower shop when she decided it might be fun to join a local acting workshop for lessons and community theater performances. She immediately enjoyed her fellow budding actors, as well as her classes and her experiences on stage in several small productions. Although the time commitment required was more than she had anticipated, she managed by cutting back a bit at work and setting aside some of her hobbies and volunteer work. Much to her surprise, she was discovered! A director friend of her acting coach came to a rehearsal and soon hired her for a small role in a production in Chicago. A year later, no longer working at the flower shop, she was balancing a busy schedule of television commercial tapings and theater performances while moving from her suburban home into an apartment downtown.

While the path to a new lifestyle is rarely without potholes, it can be traveled with success. And it often starts with a decision to jump into a major new hobby or educational experience. Here are some examples of endeavors that could spark your new lifestyle:

- **Take up a serious sport with a serious goal** (train for a biathlon or marathon, learn to race sailboats, climb a mountain, train for long-distance bicycle rides, or swim competitively)

- **Undertake social activism** (run for office, start an interest group, or manage a political campaign)

- **Pursue creative goals** (make a significant commitment to learning and practicing sculpting, acting, painting, singing, or playing a musical instrument)

- **Work toward educational achievements** (go back to college to start or finish a degree or take vocational courses toward certification in a new field of work)

All these activities require a substantial investment of time and energy, and, because they immediately put you in the company of new people and in new environments, they may eventually lead to a very different lifestyle from the one you are accustomed to.

~

As a little girl, I always wanted a horse.
So after my husband died and my kids moved away,
I bought one and began boarding her at a big horse barn out
in the country. What a time and money commitment! I had
no idea. But I also had no idea how much I could bond with an
animal and how many fascinating cowboys would be hanging
around that barn. It's a different culture out there. Now
I'm thinking of getting into breeding horses and maybe
starting my own boarding stable.

—ELISA, 60, ACCOUNTANT

~

What's in a Place?

No single undertaking has as much potential to cement a new lifestyle as relocation, whether to a new part of town or a new part of the country. Think about it: Is your current residence, especially if you have been living there for the last dozen years or more, really right for you now? Your former life likely revolved around the school district, the backyard, the garden, and the garage full of tools. Your current life, however, is less about nesting and more about lifting off the launch pad. It is about restaurants, travel, and a low-maintenance yard planted in ground cover. Or maybe your former life was consumed with your work, and you lived in a small apartment surrounded by neighbors you never met. Now you are ready to upgrade to a townhouse in a better part of town with neighbors whose interests are similar to yours.

You know you are ready for a move to a new residence if:

$\diamond$ More than 20 percent of the homes on your street have trampolines or swing sets in the backyard.

$\diamond$ You have taken and kept the business cards of two real estate agents you met in the past year.

$\diamond$ You find yourself reading the real estate section of the Sunday paper.

$\diamond$ Your yard has needed resodding for the past two years, but you haven't bothered.

$\diamond$ You live in a part of town or the country that has only mediocre real estate investment potential.

◇ Fewer than 20 percent of the apartments in your building or the homes on your street are occupied by single people of middle age and above.

◇ You are located five or ten minutes from supermarkets and home improvement emporiums, but nowhere near a good restaurant or a good bookstore.

◇ You have still not divested yourself of your son's bunk bed, your daughter's canopy bed, or the three chafing dishes you received as wedding gifts.

◇ You feel envious when you meet a single woman of about your age who has managed to move to a new location.

Relocation is the best thing that happens to a lot of single women. Almost every exemplary woman mentioned in this book, selected for successfully confronting single life after fifty, moved to a new residence not long after becoming single or turning fifty. A few moved because of a new job, but most moved because they wanted a new lease on life. They understood that they could not possibly enter a relationship with a man until they established a home that reflected their new circumstances and allowed them to look forward to the challenges ahead. Those who were most satisfied with their new locations, whether they were a mile away from their original homes or several states away, shared experiences that we used to compile the following guidelines for considering and undertaking a relocation:

- **Flock together with birds of your feather:** Choose the side of town, neighborhood, or even bedroom community that draws a high percentage of people who are single and fifty-something. Often, there are vital parts of an inner city that attract empty nesters who enjoy being close to good restaurants and theaters. Some lakeside neighborhoods and tiny villages outside larger cities do the same. If you are not moving far away from your original home, you may already have a feel for the demographic profiles of various areas. If you are, however, the local chamber of commerce or board of realtors should be able to provide community profile data.

- **Keep it simple.** Now that you're single you'll want to be able to go places and do things. Don't let yourself be seduced by the darling cottage that will tie you to its sagging front porch with demands for yard work and general upkeep. Some homes are just naturally high-maintenance. Their siding grows mold in the wink of an eye; their flower beds succumb to weeds if left briefly untended; and their pipes freeze if unused over a long weekend in January. Avoid these threats to your independence; don't make your next residence a full-time job.

- **Keep it small.** Unless you are planning on taking in boarders—which would violate the rule to keep it simple—you don't need to make a grand statement with an oversized castle. Find a place with enough room for your grown children to feel comfortable on a visit, but not so much that they will want to take over an entire wing for their own families. Keeping it small may mean saying goodbye to some of your furnishings, but this actually creates a great opportunity for you to get rid of what needs to be jettisoned anyway. Suddenly, you will find you can vacuum your entire house in ten minutes! And then you can go out and play.

- **Upscale to increase your investment potential.** If you are buying a house or condominium, stretch your finances to purchase a home in a hot area with great investment potential. This is likely to be a location that has seen substantial increases in home values over the past three to five years but has not topped out yet. Luckily, that often means an area that attracts retiring baby boomers—people whose age makes them perfect neighbors for you. Stacks of books address investing in real estate, so do some research on how to identify good investments. Why not live well and make money at the same time?

- **Call on your support network.** Relocating can be lonely. Suddenly you are surrounded by neighbors who are strangers, and your bed seems like it is at the wrong end of the house. This is the time to remember the network of family and friends you have nurtured. Some might help you pack and haul. Others might be enlisted to come over

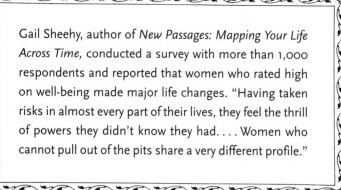

Gail Sheehy, author of *New Passages: Mapping Your Life Across Time,* conducted a survey with more than 1,000 respondents and reported that women who rated high on well-being made major life changes. "Having taken risks in almost every part of their lives, they feel the thrill of powers they didn't know they had. . . . Women who cannot pull out of the pits share a very different profile."

the day after your move and help you decide where to locate your loveseats and your antique coatrack. Emilie helped Katherine pack boxes and hang towel bars and shower curtains. Then, Katherine's friend Pam came by to tell them they had arranged the furniture all wrong!

The Bottom Line

The major changes we suggest in this chapter can only happen when you have set yourself up for success. You do that by nurturing a supportive team of family and friends. You further your success potential by taking small actions that test the waters before a big plunge—the change that at first seems risky or just too big. After the plunge, you will surface as a new you with optimism and energy—exactly the qualities that Tom, Dick, and Harry are out there hoping to find in a woman.

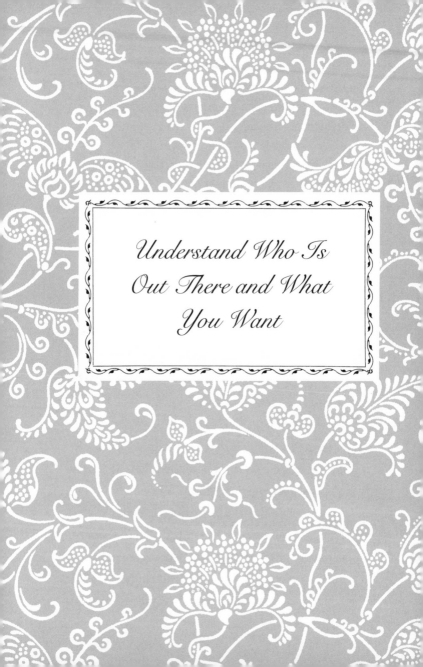

*Understand Who Is
Out There and What
You Want*

STEP

3

Define and Conquer

*M*ost of us wouldn't even think of plunging into the fray of a Victoria's Secret semiannual sale without some idea of whether we were searching for panties, bras, or nighties. The numerous piles of marked-down items, continually churned by dozens of hands reaching in from every direction, are just too daunting if you haven't yet decided if you need pink or black, cotton or silk, small or large. But, if you know what you want, you're likely to get what you came for: savings galore.

This is, of course, a metaphor for intentional action: in relationships and in life, you are more likely to find it if you're looking for it—as long as you can describe exactly what "it" is. In this case, it's necessary to discover what it is that you seek in a relationship and, consequently, in a man. In other words, determining the kind of relationship you want and the future you envision for yourself will help you define the guy who is right for you. Although math was never our specialty, we came up with the following formula for finding the right man:

YOUR RELATIONSHIP NEEDS

+ YOUR VISION OF YOUR FUTURE LIFESTYLE

= THE MAN YOU INTEND TO FIND

Note that this equation puts the man *after* your lifestyle and relationship preferences. You don't stumble across a guy one day and then reconstruct your notions about the kind of relationship and future you want so that they will match his agenda. That approach is a whopping big time waster, because it may take a year or more for you to confront and deal with the reality that you lost the "you" in that relationship. If you understand what kind of relationship suits you and what sort of future you want, then you will know the kind of man you need to find. And you will be far more likely to find him.

Reversing the equation and putting the man before your needs and your vision is a very common mistake that has entangled many smart and experienced women, including both of us. But you can be smarter than smart. Consider the following consequences of getting into a relationship with the wrong guy:

🌱 **Frustrating Flirtations:** You forgot that you wanted "from this day forward" when you took up with a perennial playboy.

🌱 **Speed Bumps:** He's already planted his wing tips in your closet, but you are still in enjoy-the-moment mode.

🌱 **Scratchless Itches:** Your candles and bubble bath are petrifying in the pantry, while he uses you as a dinner partner only.

🌱 **Unhappenings:** He's still around, still yours . . . and still uncommitted.

🌱 **Clogged Drains:** His slow route to romance fits your preference for a warm and caring friendship, but turns downright chilly when the hugs become high fives and the conversations are only about the weather.

🌱 **Castaways:** Your long-distance relationship includes great weekends from time to time, but he has no interest in communicating in between.

Women who know what they want and move with intention have a good chance of avoiding these time-wasting, thoroughly aggravating relationships. This requires that you define the sort of relationship and the future you want for yourself, whether it includes close friendships, brief romantic flings, or a long-term partnership. Then, you can specify the kind of man, or men, who are just right for you.

I kept praying to God to send me a good man,
and soon good men were falling from the sky, but they were
the wrong men! Then I prayed to God to send me a widower who'd
had a good marriage. The next thing I knew I met Ted, a widower
who'd had a good marriage. He turned out to be the right man.
You know, you have to be specific when you pray.

—LINDA SUE, 58, MARKETING EXECUTIVE

The Right Relationship—for You

The leader of any enterprise or group will tell you that strategy counts. First you must define your mission and your goals, and eventually they will guide your actions to accomplish them. The mission is your statement of intention; the goals are more specific descriptions of what you intend will happen and when.

Having clear intentions allows you to pursue a relationship with a man strategically. To lack a clear intent is to be wishy-washy—to stare in confusion at the mountain of silky items at that lingerie sale and to walk away empty-handed. An intentional statement about a relationship is specific: "I want to develop a relationship with a man who is a friend and secondarily (if at all) a lover, but who mostly wants to do active, outdoorsy things with me and to make me laugh."

A statement lacking intention is vague: "I really want a guy around who cares about me." The first statement can lead to finding the right man. The second is more likely to lead to confusion about how to start or to frustrating relationships that are liable to fail.

It's not all that difficult to pinpoint the kind of relationship or relationships that you want, because there are only a finite number of options. Most of the questions you ask yourself should focus on compatibility with your needs. Answering the following survey requires you to reflect on what you want in a relationship in many areas where compatibility is an issue. Place an X in the column that indicates how you feel about each of the following statements.

Keep the results—possibly tuck a copy in your underwear drawer—and use them as inspiration to help you avoid or leave a relationship that isn't happening. If you are not the survey-taking type, at least do what our friend Carrie did when she was deciding whether to continue her three-month relationship with Dan. She simply wrote a list of every feature she wanted in an ideal relationship and then put stars by those she was likely to get with Dan. Her thirteen-item list had only two stars—not a good showing for Dan.

Another alternative is to pinpoint your current preferences on a continuum of relationship possibilities. At one end is platonic friendship; at the other is full-time live-in commitment. First, think about what you want now. Then, think about what

DEFINITELY	SOMEWHAT	NOT AT ALL	**In the Relationship I Want . . .**
			We will be together most of our waking hours.
			We will like the same recreational activities.
			Good and frequent sex will be an important part of the relationship.
			Companionship will be more important than romance.
			We will just be good friends.
			We will be very romantic, with lots of kisses and endearments.
			We will be very busy with travel, recreation, and our social life.
			We will mostly have quiet togetherness, close to home.
			We will quickly commit to only each other.
			We will see each other, but not exclusively.
			We will marry.
			We will live together but not marry.
			We will keep our separate residences.
			We will not see each other every day.
			We will each have our own friends and interests.
			A long-distance relationship is okay.
			We will share expenses equally in everything we do.
			He will pay for the things we do together.
			We will integrate our finances.
			We will both want to be very involved with our grown children, who will blend as one family.

you intend for five or ten years from now. The choices look like this:

- **Platonic friendships:** You have one or more brotherly pals.

- **Dating companionships:** You go out, but just for social companionship.

- **Feel-good flings:** You go out and enjoy occasional flirting and/or intimacy.

- **Real romance:** You spend a lot of time and develop real intimacy with one special man.

- **Commitment:** You decide to live together and build a future.

The more you arm yourself with information about what you really want in a relationship, the more likely you are to adhere to your own desires as you meet men who may or may not want the same kind of relationship. We are not about to tell you what kind of relationship you should want, only that the relationship you get should be the one you want.

If all this seems easier said than done, well, of course it is! Long ago, when we were proud to own our first padded bras and a couple of LPs, we learned to keep our preferences in check. We felt lucky just to have a date on a Saturday night, so why get picky? Our mothers told us that even if a blind date turned out to be a zero, complete with bad breath and a pocket protector, we should be kind, cheerful, gracious, and sweet.

We can both still hear our mom advising us, "Even if you can't stand him, you have a responsibility to make sure he has a good time. And he might have friends." We stored away our own desires and simply coped in silence. After affairs and marriage, many women have become resigned to the idea that relationships are never perfect, and as a result some of us are willing to accept a lot less than we want—and a lot less than we deserve.

Thanks to your years of experience and a steady diet of feminist ideology, you are past that now. Or you should be. Old habits are hard to break, so arm yourself against being pulled in the wrong direction by knowing exactly who you are and what you need from others. If you get drawn off course, make a correction in the direction of what you know about yourself and your preferences, needs, hopes, and dreams.

Transitional Relationships—When Less Is More

There is one exception to our rule that all relationships require self-knowledge and intention, and that is the "transitional relationship." This very short-term friendship or fling is enjoyable without having any potential for duration. It is good for keeping the cobwebs out of your mind (and other places) while you are making plans for a real relationship.

The transitional man is a placeholder—someone to simply keep you busy until what you really want comes along. He is not someone you want to see often or for very long; and, hopefully, he sees you in a similar light. You have no desire to give him long-term support for getting over his divorce or to cry on his shoulder about your lousy job. The transitional relationship may be superficial, but it has its purpose and can be interesting and fun. Enjoy it, but keep your eyes wide open and don't lose sight of other possibilities on the horizon. Good prospects for transitional relationships include:

- A man who is first enjoying dating after a disappointing divorce

- A man who lives more than a thousand miles away

- A man who is so busy with work and other interests that he can only see you once a week

- A man who is moving out of town in a few months

- A man who is fun to be around but has a romantic relationship with a woman who lives in another town

These men are generally in situations that cause your relationship to wind down on its own after a period of time—which is exactly what is supposed to happen in a transitional relationship. Temporary is not a bad thing, as long as you are both honest about it. Neither party in a transitional relationship should have expectations about the future.

Trading in Futures—Your Own

If you want a relationship with legs—one that will last into the next ten or more years—it is a good idea to clarify for yourself what you want your life to look like in the future. Think of that future life as a way of being that does not start or end with the relationship or the man. It is *your* future way of being, which hopefully will be supported and enriched by a fulfilling relationship or multiple relationships.

The future you will have is, of course, as predictable as the weather or a teenager's moods. However, you are much more likely to get the future you want if you set an intention. What do you want your future to look like? What goals do you want to achieve? Do you want to become a competitive senior swimmer? Do you want to visit the Greek Islands? Do you want to write a book? Do you want to diet and exercise so that you look good in a tank top? Do you want to learn and use sign language? Researchers on aging agree that setting life goals and striving toward them favorably affect physical and mental well-being. Setting these goals can also help develop fulfilling relationships with men.

You'll want to set at least two types of goals: action goals, or what you want to achieve, and life pattern goals, or how you want to live. Action goals might include new endeavors, changes in your habits, or doing more or less of the things you already do. These are your "to do" goals. Life pattern goals address the amount of time and energy you want to spend in

When Syracuse University researchers Anne Gauthier and Timothy Smeeding examined the time use patterns of people from age fifty-five to sixty-four, they found that the daily patterns of retired people were very similar to their patterns of time use on weekends when they were employed, with a slight adjustment toward more time spent on passive leisure activities and less time on active leisure activities.

different areas of your life, from loafing on the couch to professional development to volunteer work. To get clear about both types of goals, put them in writing, listing your top three to five goals of each type. For action goals, consider travel, learning opportunities, professional endeavors, and self-improvement. For life pattern goals, consider how you'd like to spend each day. For example, your goals might include doing more paid work, more social leisure activities, more active leisure activities, fewer passive leisure activities, less volunteer work, and less housework and home maintenance.

A successful relationship with the man who is right for you will match your action goals and your life pattern goals. He's probably not right for you if the daily routine he prefers involves quietly dangling a line at his favorite fishing hole and napping before dinner while you want a companion for an active social life. There might be a way to compromise on your goals, but determine this before you get too involved to easily extricate yourself.

A Beautiful Find

So how do you determine who is Mr. Right? He could come from any location, any profession, and any background. The possibilities are nearly endless, and endlessly confusing. But, just as it is useful for you to determine in advance what you want your life to look like in the future, it also helps to know what you want in a man before you start looking. Maybe you just can't deal with someone who is a lot younger than you, or someone who is not as physically vigorous or as socially active. If you are able to arm yourself in advance by determining what traits are important to you in a man, you are less likely to waste time on Mr. Wrong and more likely to put yourself in the path of Mr. Right.

Think like a high-level manager who is hiring a new assistant for a position she just created. A competent manager will not even begin to look for her assistant until she clarifies what she is looking for: the responsibilities and duties she needs the assistant to accomplish, the experience and knowledge she wants the assistant to bring to the job, and the individual attributes that will best fit with the rest of the team. Only then is she ready to write a description of qualities she is seeking, to publicize that description in appropriate places, and to sort through applications from hopeful candidates. This process is similar to the search for Mr. Right. You can narrow the field by knowing what kind of individual you are seeking. Although you will still need to "interview" a lot of candidates, including a fair share of frogs who will never morph into princes, your initial written description is a valuable tool in your search.

When we asked women in successful relationships about how they found their men, many admitted to a great deal of trial and error. They discovered what sort of men they wanted only after they found what was missing or what they appreciated in those they met. Some also noted that they made snap judgments when deciding whether to respond to men who seemed interested. Looks and opening lines could lead to quick exits or quick interest. However, the women who established solid and satisfying relationships fairly quickly and experienced the least frustration with relationships that turned sour were those who reported knowing what they were looking for at the outset.

~

I've been through two marriages that ended
in divorce and a string of male friendships and romances
that started when I was fifteen years old. I think by now
I know what my Mr. Right looks like, thinks like,
acts like, and even smells like.

—MARILYN, 61, CORPORATE EXECUTIVE

~

Experience and knowledge are two benefits that come with advancing years. Use them to your advantage by reflecting on men you have known. What did they do that worked or didn't work for you? What qualities in a man have made you feel good about him . . . and about you, too? Which characteristics made you want to see more of a man? Which made you want to never see him again?

After some general reflection, organize your thoughts. Grab a pen and divide a sheet of paper into two columns. At the top of one write "Desired Characteristics." At the top of the other, write "Desired Behaviors." List your preferences for the right guy under each.

Characteristics That Count

Characteristics are factors inherent in the individual and his life: his age, appearance, intelligence, health, financial situation, and even his geographical location. Ask yourself questions about what qualities you want in all these areas.

AGE

When a man over fifty says he is seeing "an older woman," he generally means one who is two to five years younger than himself. He almost never describes himself as seeing "a younger woman," even if she is a contemporary of his first grandchild, because that situation is too commonplace to merit mentioning. However, a woman over fifty may choose to be with "an older man" who really is older, or "a younger man" of five to fifteen (or more) years her junior. Are you open to a wide range of possibilities, or do you decidedly prefer men of a certain age?

Ask yourself about the younger man:

- Will he make you feel old?

- Will he make you suspicious about his motives?

- Will he make you feel guilty if you can't keep up with his active lifestyle?

- Will you feel unwanted pressure to look and act younger yourself?

- Will he bring out the best in you, giving you the boost you need to stay active, look your best, and enjoy a busy life?

Ask yourself about the older man:

- Are you ready to sympathize with his aches and pains?

- Can you deal with male menopause, which ushers in everything from anxiety and diminished sex drive to an enlarged prostate and hair growth in odd places?

- Will his primary need for tender companionship match your need for the same?

- Will he make you feel old?

- Will you have the patience for his growing fretfulness, grumpiness, conservatism, and hypochondria?

- ❧ Will his lifestyle mesh nicely with your need for a less active lifestyle and a care-giving relationship?

LOOKS

If thinking about what you'd like the man in your life to look like makes you feel a bit superficial, consider this: men aren't viewed as shallow because they know they wouldn't be happy with a 300-pound woman sprouting hair above her upper lip. Men are more likely than women to have very specific preferences for the appearance of the person they date, right down to breast size and ankle diameter. Many women also have preferences, and that's not a bad thing—it's just part of knowing yourself and what you want. Ask yourself:

- ❧ Can you be with a very short man or a very fat man?

- ❧ Do you shy away from baldness or from transplanted hair that doesn't ever quite seem to grow into a single mass?

- ❧ Do you draw the line at a large belly or a sunken chest?

- ❧ Are muscles, or at least firmness, a preference?

- ❧ Does race matter?

INTELLIGENCE

This is one area where you could easily miss out on a guy with real soul mate potential if you don't remain flexible. There are many types of intelligence, including scholarly intellect, street smarts, emotional intelligence, and the ability to learn quickly.

Maybe the emotionally solid guy, with a quiet knowledge of who he is and what he wants, does not have an encyclopedic vocabulary or four college degrees. But, if you are a scholarly genius who happens to be a drama queen, he may be an ideal partner for you. You can do the Sunday *New York Times* crossword puzzle in fifteen minutes flat, but you forget to change the oil in your car. He remembers the oil and changes it himself, but he can't come up with a three-letter acronym for "failed constitutional amendment." What could be better? When thinking about the intelligence you want your partner to have, don't think simply in terms of little or lots. Think about the different ways in which you need him to be intelligent and ask yourself:

- What *kind* of intelligences does he need to have?

- What does he have to do to be "smart"?

- Can you deal with someone whom you would describe as not as intelligent as you are?

- In what ways do you lack intelligence, and how might you choose a man who complements you best?

HEALTH

Although it's impossible to know what the future will bring in terms of your own health and that of your potential partners, you can at least reflect on the possible outcomes and how you feel about each of them. Sometimes his less-than-perfect health can bring out your nurturing side. But maybe you don't have a nurturing side, or perhaps you expended your desire to nurture on your children or your former spouse. Maybe now you would prefer someone who can deal patiently and empathetically with your own health needs. Ask yourself the following questions:

- Must he be hearty and fit now and for the foreseeable future?

- Will you have the patience to hear about one physical complaint after another? Can you deal with hypochondria?

- Can you deal with someone who had recent prostate surgery? Who recently recovered from a small stroke? Whose family has a history of Alzheimer's?

- How do you feel about the possibility of becoming a nurse at some point? Pushing a wheelchair? Doing all the work?

- Will you want to support him through the ups and downs of depression, anxiety, or other mental disorders?

- Will some of his health issues make you feel needed in a good way?

- How will you need him to react to your health issues?

MONEY

The centerpiece of the perfect trio of characteristics, "healthy, wealthy, and wise," is a touchy subject. But, because the activities you participate in and the lifestyle you enjoy are in part a consequence of your financial situation, you shouldn't be afraid to address it. Ask yourself:

- Can you be with someone who cannot support you, someone who wants, or perhaps needs, you each to pay your own way?

- Will you be embarrassed when someone spends too lavishly on you?

- Will the miserly mister make you fume?

- Are you looking for someone who will enable you to upscale your lifestyle by taking you to expensive places and giving you lavish presents?

- Would you prefer to be financial equals who financially contribute to the relationship at about the same rate?

- Would you enjoy being in a better financial position than your ideal man so that you can "do nice things" for him?

LOCATION, LOCATION, LOCATION

Typically, men—especially men who don't want to invest energy in the day-to-day necessities of a relationship—are better than women at long-distance relationships. Some long-distance associations are ideal for the needs of one partner but not so ideal for the other. You can exchange letters, you can email, but you can't cuddle at a distance of 200 miles. You can have sexy phone conversations, but something is missing. He can't be your escort or your companion most of the time. To avoid frustration, think about what you need and how often you need a man to be available to you. Long-distance interactions can work well if you are very independent, or if you want a man (or men) somewhere in your life but don't necessarily want a full-time relationship. Figure out what your needs are now—before you commit to the commute.

- Are you okay with a long-distance relationship, but only if you see each other most weekends?

- Would you be happy with one great long weekend each month? Or one great week every several months?

- Do your own unpredictable schedule and independent outlook make a long-distance relationship especially attractive?

- Is a long-distance relationship ideal for now because you just need a transitional relationship while you are settling into a new stage of life?

- Does your need to be touched, to be held, to be told you smell good mean you're not suited to a long-distance relationship?

- Does it make you crazy to wait for the next phone call or the return email?

On His Best Behavior

His behaviors show up as his personal style and demeanor; they are related to his style of communication, his empathy, his humor, his orientation toward action, his sense of adventure, and his sense of romance. Ask yourself questions about what you want in all these areas.

COMMUNICATION STYLE

It should come as no surprise that men typically communicate very differently than women. Most men communicate more concisely, more directly, and less frequently than women, who often find casual conversation natural and fun. However, it can be disquieting to be with a very quiet man or jarring to be with the rare male jabberer. Consider the style of communication that suits you best.

- Do quiet men strike you as disinterested and boring? Or do they seem to you thoughtful and reflective?

- Do you get irritated by very talkative men who seem to hog the conversational airtime? Or do you enjoy the opportunity to sit back and listen?

- Will his lively and expansive style as life of the party set you on edge? Or will it provide the entertainment you are looking for?

- How much does he need to be able to make you laugh?

- Are you okay with someone who never calls just to say "Hi, how are you?"?

- Does he really need to converse with you? Or is it okay if he just reads the sports section while you talk?

- Can you deal with two-word responses to your three-paragraph email messages?

ACTIVITY LEVEL

If you enjoy an active life full of fitness classes and racquetball matches, you may prefer a partner who can join in on the fun, or simply be at home when you come in to collapse. On the other hand, you may be fairly inactive but would enjoy the motivation provided by an active and adventuresome partner. Ask yourself:

- Does a sedentary man seem like a lazy couch potato to you?

- Will you get bored if he would rather stay home than join you in outdoor activities?

- Will his high energy get on your nerves?

- Will you enjoy life more if someone inspires you with his sense of adventure and active pursuits?

- Are there any specific activities that you will want him to pursue with you?

EMOTIONAL STYLE

It may be a myth that men are less emotional than women, but it is clear they don't express the same emotions in the same ways. A few men are truly emotionally challenged to the point of chronic insensitivity. Some women are okay with that, but we're pretty certain we haven't met any of them. Most of us want to sense an emotional connection with the men who are our friends or lovers. If you crave warmth, you don't want a guy who never talks to his dog, never compliments you, and never asks about your terminally ill mother. If he doesn't have even a basic ability to express his emotions, he doesn't deserve you, even for a temporary fling. On the other hand, you may be grateful for a man's emotional equanimity when you're suffering your own dramatic meltdown about an unexpected disaster. Since we all need varying degrees of emotional expression, ask yourself:

- Do you need him to remember every holiday and birthday, or are some lapses excusable?

- Will you feel brushed off if he doesn't empathize with your latest auto repair nightmare or notice your new hair color?

- Will you appreciate his cool head and rational approach to situations that make you feel stressed and anxious?

- Will your ego suffer if he rarely (or never) tells you how good you look, feel, and smell?

- Can you deal with intense emotions on his part, like anxiety, depression, or grief?

- Will you enjoy a relationship where there are no displays of anger, jealousy, irritation, or impatience?

Chemistry

All of the foregoing considerations are irrelevant without chemistry. We are very big fans of the rush and the flush—that all-over good feeling you get when you are just downright attracted to someone, even if only as a great pal, for no reason that you can express. Chemistry will trump your carefully constructed intentions every time, with consequences that might be very good . . . or very bad. We can't tell you to ignore chemistry and use your head; we know that it's not always possible. But we can tell you that if you use your head first, you might be able to get all the qualities you're looking for in a man *and* enjoy a chemical attraction at the same time.

Chemical and biological researchers have long known that pheromones, chemical substances produced and secreted by humans and other animals, serve to stimulate emotional and behavioral responses such as physical attraction or revulsion. You meet someone and find yourself intensely drawn to him for reasons you cannot describe. You feel excited and delighted just to be around him. If he reciprocates, you are joyous. Even if he is everything you were *not* looking for in a man and wants everything you *don't* want in a relationship, you are in a state of rapture.

We can't tell you not to go there, because this chemical attraction plays by its own set of rules. Just keep all the lists you made as you read this chapter close at hand so that you can eventually say, "No wonder this seems so perfect" or "I see why this isn't going to work out." You will be able to bask in well-deserved satisfaction or make a new start that relies on your well-defined intentions to discover the next chemically attractive man.

Clearly, this step of defining your needs and wants requires more reflection than action. You need to think about yourself and about the many kinds of men, relationships, and lifestyles that are available to you. Asking specific questions, such as those we have included here, will help. Putting your thoughts in writing, as we'll ask you to do at the conclusion of this book, will give you the ammunition you need to find the relationship that's right for you.

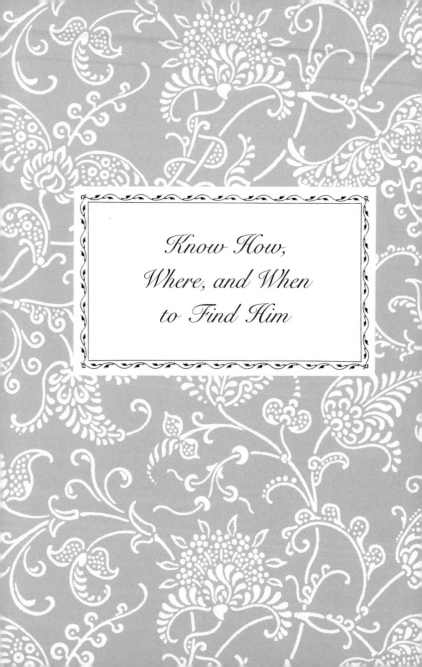

Know How,
Where, and When
to Find Him

MOVE INTO VIEW—HIS

*W*HEN YOU KNOW WHAT KIND of relationship you are looking for, it should be easy to spot the right kind of guy and move into his orbit, right? But, as we know all too well, it's not. Men come in too many shapes, sizes, and states of mind, and many contradictory qualities can be lodged in one fellow. So get ready for the unexpected:

- The paunchy friend with the sunny demeanor seems great for brotherly hugs and silly times at a NASCAR race. Turns out he'd rather stay home on Sunday and do the *New York Times* crossword puzzle with you.

- The square-jawed silvering stud with big hands and part ownership in a race horse wonders if you'd be interested in taking salsa dancing lessons.

❧ The workaholic dentist with frumpy clothes and baggy eyes is decidedly conversationally challenged to boot, but your knees go weak the first time he touches you below the chin.

You just never know where you're going to find the man, or men, for you, which means that you need to look in many places and at many possibilities, casting the net widely into the ocean of men who might meet your needs. Let's stick with that fishing metaphor: You are out at sea looking for the big, firm tunas with real potential. You unfurl your sails and skim across the waves to a spot where they are most likely to be found. But the currents and tides push them around quite a bit, and other small, limp nontunas are mixed in with them. So, you cast the net far and wide, and when you haul it up you've got on deck several tunas and quite a few other fishy-looking specimens. You then change course toward a spot on your chart that is not such likely tuna territory, but where they might congregate to wait out a storm. You cast your net far and wide again, bringing in another mixed group. Next, you check them all out—tunas and, because they are there, the other fish, too. You never can tell. Finally, you decide which are the keepers (for now, anyway) and which you'll toss back with a plop. "Sorry, Charlie."

It's a simple process of three moves that work in nature and in life:

1. Search widely to bring in a worthy bunch

2. Check out the creatures in your net

3. Keep those that look like they might fit your needs

Because you already know your intent, you limit the chance of disaster—like checking out your catch for the wrong qualities or keeping creatures you should have quickly jettisoned. But, you still have to cast that net.

The Virtue of Volume

Since you never know exactly when or where you might bump into the right guy for you, commit to investigating a large number of prospective venues—even ones that seem to have very little potential. Volume is your best friend in the search for any man, whether he's an occasional dinner party companion or a long-term mate.

The women who are the most successful at finding men are the most active. They join clubs and groups, sing in their church choirs, walk their neighbors' dogs, attend wine tastings, volunteer, and compete in 3K charity runs. They consistently put themselves in the path of many people, including men who might be the one they're looking for *and* other men and women who might guide them to the right man.

Search constantly, and search everywhere. Set volume goals: meeting one or two prequalified (that is, definitely available) new men each month is a good minimum. Persist. Know that the person you will really click with is out there, but he doesn't live next door, and his daily path doesn't cross your current daily path. You need to reach beyond the patterns of your usual life in order to discover him—and let him discover you. Get some new interests, get energized, get several really good pairs of shoes, and get going.

The Get Moving Creed

(Developed by Emilie and successfully tested by Katherine and twelve of our single friends)

Whenever I can be out, I don't stay in. He is not the UPS delivery guy about to arrive on your doorstep. Those guys are by definition too young, because you have to be very young to look good in tree toad brown. Get out the door and into the world.

Whenever I get an invitation, I accept it. Even if it is an invite from the loser who dumped your best friend last week, if it puts you in the company of other people, go!

Whenever I have an opportunity to join something, I join it. Join a writers' group, a book club, a mall-walking group, a church, or a synagogue. The other joiners may not seem like your type, but they can still lead you to their more inspiring acquaintances.

Whenever I get a chance to try something new that interests me, I do it. Go surf casting; go to Bermuda; go to

a blues festival or a film festival. Buy a sports car. Adopt a
dog. Learn tap dancing. You'll become more interesting, and
you'll meet interesting new people.

Places You Go and People You Meet

Recently divorced Anna met Don when they both brought
their new dogs to puppy training classes. Teresa, caught in the
middle of a four-car fender bender on her way to a museum
opening, vaguely recalled Mario as a long-ago neighbor when
he stopped to help. Sarah was flying to parents' weekend at
her daughter's college when she met Bill during a delay that
grounded their plane on the runway for two hours. Connie
met Gerald while visiting her parents in Iowa.

All these meetings resulted in good short- or long-term
relationships. None would have happened without things to do
and places to go. In order to meet more potential partners,
however, you also need to deliberately seek out additional activities. Start with activities that both interest you *and* will land
you in the orbit of available men of the appropriate age. You
will be actively engaged in new endeavors that appeal to you,
which is a huge plus all by itself, and your activities will help
you meet your relationship goals.

Your Best Bets: Check Them Off

The following checklist offers activities aimed at meeting more people. Some might be things you already do or places you already frequent. Concentrate on the things you don't already do, especially those things you've always wanted to do but never tried. Do something new every week for at least the next two months. Then, add your own ideas to the list.

MENTAL EXERCISES

◇ Go to your local library.

◇ Attend art gallery openings.

◇ Prowl through museums.

◇ Attend lectures.

◇ Enjoy symphonies, concerts, theater, or operas.

◇ Shop or browse at bookstores or attend author readings.

◇ Add your own ideas here:

PHYSICAL EXERCISES

◇ Learn a new sport, such as fly fishing, golf, tennis, or sailing.

◇ Join a sports group, such as a golf team, tennis team, or bicycle touring group.

◇ Travel for adventure.

◇ Attend sporting events.

◇ Spend mornings or early evenings at a fitness club.

◇ Jog or power walk.

◇ Bicycle (safely, on designated trails or bicycle paths).

◇ Add your own ideas here:

ACTIVE LEISURE PURSUITS

◇ Walk a dog in the park.

◇ Attend wine tastings.

◇ Join the darts game at your local bar.

◇ Join in charity walks.

◇ Add your own ideas here:

GROUP ACTIVITIES

◇ Take courses to learn new things, such as cooking, bicycle or car repair, consumer law, computer programs, pottery, or photography.

◇ Sign up for a degree or certificate program at the local college.

◇ Join a group, such as a writing or photography workshop, a book club, a dinner club, or a dance group.

◇ Attend church or synagogue, perhaps joining the finance board or the choir or participating in volunteer activities.

◇ Volunteer for a political campaign, an educational endeavor, or a food bank.

◇ Add your own ideas here:

AND DON'T FORGET

◇ Attend class reunions.

◇ Attend weddings and funerals.

◇ Join in neighborhood clean-up weekends.

◇ Attend local festivals and parades.

◇ Hang out at coffeehouses and hardware stores.

◇ Add your own ideas here:

We also like to stay keenly aware of improved net casting as we go about our daily routines. You can do all the things you usually do —-perhaps with a new activity salted in once a week or so—while continually being alert for new male associations.

～◡

*After my divorce I decided to take an acting class just for fun.
I met lots of fascinating men in that class, but no one I wanted
to spend a whole lot more time with. Then, while I was sitting at
Starbucks studying a script one afternoon, I met Ron, a wonderful
man who had nothing to do with acting. We dated for almost
a year and are still good friends.*

—LAURA, 59, PART-TIME ACTOR

Opportunity Around the Corner

You don't always need to vary your routines by much in order to put yourself in the path of interesting men. Make slight changes to when and where you perform your routine activities and you'll improve your chances of landing in the path of appropriate guys doing the same things.

Beverly's Strategic Supermarketing

When our friend Beverly in Washington, D.C., skidded into divorce as a fifty-four-year-old accountant, she remembered an old haunt from her single days, the "social Safeway" supermarket in Georgetown, where many men and women made weekend plans while shopping Friday evening. With her usual cool head, she notes, "I had to grocery shop anyway, so I figured I might as well do it where I could meet, or even just watch, interesting people." Beverly began shopping there again, even though it was half an hour from her home. No luck. After four visits among aisles of singles half her age, she reconsidered where the more mature crowd might shop. She settled upon the Watergate Safeway, on the ground level of that venerable building, and bingo! She immediately started having interesting conversations while waiting in line and soon snagged a date with Phil, who eventually introduced her to Allen, now her significant other.

Beverly's experience reminds us that even when you do reach out, sometimes you will still end up with nothing. There are many different routes to the same place, and some take you on detours. If necessary, plot another route. Beverly needed to regroup and reroute, and her persistence paid off.

DOUBLE TAKES: OLD FLAMES REDISCOVERED

Even while meeting new men, you can't help but wonder whatever happened to Tom? Or Jim? Or Peter? Or any of those young studs you adored in high school, in college, between marriages, or—it happens—during marriage? We all have some fond memories of guys whom we loved, left (okay, some left us), and never really forgot. Where has he been since you returned his letter sweater and traipsed off to college? What happened to him after you marched arm in arm during antiwar demonstrations? You heard he married, became a Wall Street wizard, and moved to Connecticut; but then what? He didn't show up at the class reunion, but the reunion directory gave his phone number and address. Do you dare?

Of course you dare! This is a person with whom you once had chemistry, so why leave it languishing in the beaker? You know a lot more about him than about someone you just met for the first time at midlife or beyond. And even if you haven't seen him in thirty years, you know something about his character, his education, his friends, his family, and his personality.

What You Do	How You Do It
Grocery shopping	Right after work, preferably on Friday, at a store located in single male territory.
Working out	At a good co-ed club, after work during busy hours. Don't take classes, unless they are the rare ones that attract men. Otherwise, just use the weights and machines.
Reading	On Sunday at a café or on a park bench.
Walking	In a park, with a dog (borrowed if necessary) that likes to make friends with other dogs.
Power walking or jogging	Saturday morning or Sunday afternoon on well-traveled public trails or on the beach. Consider joining a running group for people of your ability and age.
Eating breakfast	On the way to work, at a busy café or a bagel shop.
Eating lunch	In open places, like in the middle of the restaurant or on park bench, and never at your desk or in a restaurant corner.
Home maintenance shopping	At big home improvement stores on the weekends. Linger in the tool section; check out the cordless drills. Skip the patio and garden sections.

You don't know if he is available, and it is very likely he is not, but you may enjoy finding out how he is doing anyway. And if it turns out he is available, then the odds are good that some sort of chemistry might still exist.

If you need encouragement, we can provide it from first-hand experience. Shortly after her divorce, Katherine found she was gun-shy about meeting new men. The unknown was just way too scary. However, within two years she had managed to enjoy some fun times with three former boyfriends. One was a widower with whom she had kept in touch over the years; he treated her to some lovely weekend getaways. Another was a man she phoned on a whim when she was visiting the town where they both lived twenty years earlier; she discovered he had never left and never married, and the chemistry was still there. Still another was a divorced high school classmate who called after locating her through mutual friends. From these three recycled relationships, Katherine ended up with a brief fling, a long-distance romance, and a good pal—all of which helped give her the ego boost she needed to enjoy her single life.

Making Contact

Class reunions are obviously an excellent way to reconnect with men who are the appropriate age and may be available. But these opportunities only come around every so many years, and they only allow you access to a limited number

From Jilted to Joyful

Shortly after her highly publicized divorce from New York mayor Rudolph Giuliani, fifty-two-year-old Donna Hanover received a phone call from her former Stanford University classmate Edwin Oster, whom she had not spoken to in years. Was she planning to attend their thirtieth class reunion, he wondered? She decided to go, reacquainted herself with many old friends, and married Oster a year later.

of your old friends and lovers. Mutual friends are another good source for getting in touch with old flames. And thankfully we women tend to have a way of keeping in touch with a network of people, even as we move across country or beyond. Somebody in that network is likely to know the whereabouts of good ol' James.

And you can always use the Internet. Typing his name into a search engine may take you to the web site of the organization where he now works, where you might find his current resume. You might even be able to discern his marital status. Likewise, web services like Friendfinders.com can do the tracking for you.

Clearly, there is no reason for you to find him if you are going to be too shy to approach him. Fortunately, email is a big help in this area. The phone works too, but if you are bound and determined to be tongue-tied the minute he says "hello," then get his email address and write something like:

"I stumbled across your email address in the most unusual way and thought it meant I should get in touch after all these years. Let me know how and what you are doing sometime; I'd love to catch up. Of the old gang, I'm in touch only with Linda, but I do still think of everyone often. My own life here in Santa Clara is somewhat chaotic as a single lady still working way too hard in the advertising world. But, I do manage to play tennis on the weekends and to travel on occasion. I hope you'll fill me in on your own activities over the years. Take care, Marilyn."

This sort of email tells him that you're single, you're active, and you're interested in getting reacquainted. Don't dwell on your children, your parents, your health setbacks, or your former husband. He will take it from there . . . or not.

A phone call is a bit more personal and may be more effective than email or snail mail if you are checking out a possible romantic attraction. Most calls will direct you to the message machine, where you can record in a light and smiley tone: "Hi, Jeremy, this is Marilyn Jones. I think it has been about eighteen years since I've seen you, but I've recently been in touch with Paul and Linda, and we all speak of you often. I'm wondering where you are and how you're doing, so give a call sometime if you get a chance at 555-6054. Looking forward.

Thanks." Ditto on the tone and the opening sentence or two if you actually get him on the phone in person. But, we suggest you first have a glass of wine and relax in your most comfy chair or sofa.

If you want to get really creative, print up a newsletter-type Christmas note, half a page or so (nothing as long as a letter), with a recent photo of you in one corner. Let him know what you're doing and where you are, including your "new" phone and email address, while implying that this is the note you've sent to all your friends. Tuck it into a card and mention that you just came across his address.

Online Dating for Fun or for Keeps

The Internet is an incredibly handy tool for searching far and wide with just the click of a mouse. The number of men and women over fifty searching for one another with the help of online dating services is well over a million, which means that it's very likely that a good match for you has a posting somewhere in cyberspace right now. But, if you are new to the sport, you'll need to arm yourself with information.

THE SEARCH AND THE SORT

There are nearly countless profiles and photos of mature singles online, each interested in meeting a compatible individual. With information about so many candidates right at your fingertips, the challenge is to sort out the real possibilities from the duds, and to spot any fibbers or otherwise undesirable men who might cross your computer screen. Thankfully, you don't have to weed through the millions of personal profiles posted online one by one. Many web sites have sections especially for singles beyond midlife. Other sites specialize only in the over-fifty age group. Among the latter group are SilverSingles.com, SeniorsCircle.com, SeniorFriendFinder.com, SassySeniors.com, and NeverTooLate.com. Other sites, such as eHarmony.com, narrow the field for you by matching individuals based on their personality tests. You can also get help with snapping a flattering photograph and writing a good online profile at LookBetterOnline.com and ProfileDoctor.com. From E-Cyrano.com, you receive personal consultation about all aspects of Internet searching and dating.

If you have been out of circulation for a while, Internet dating can be a very good way to get started again at your own pace. You are in control, because you only talk to men you find interesting—first online, then by phone, and then in person, if you choose. Before meeting in person, you can check him out on Google, verify his place of employment, and use your intuition about his answers to questions about his past and present. There is no insult in backing away or ignoring someone who emails you, although a "no thank you" email is always considered proper etiquette.

Patty's Internet Intrigue

Our friend Patty, a fifty-two-year-old sculptor in New Mexico, knew that neither her work nor her location afforded enough opportunities for meeting eligible men. She began dating online only reluctantly when she realized that it might be the only way for her to expand her choices. "I wasn't eager to sort through frogs, but I was eager to meet someone I could share my life with. So, I selected a site that did personality matching and just jumped in," she recalls.

She soon met George, owner of his own technology company in Maryland. Warily, she asked him questions by email and phone that tested his honesty; when he answered openly and without taking offense, he became all the more attractive to her. Patty also went online to check the legitimacy of George's company and look for his name on the National Sex Offender Registry. After months of phone calls, she traveled to Maryland to meet him. She arranged her own accommodations and continued to cautiously grill the man who was now thrilling her with his polite demeanor, impressive friends, and lovely meals at his home. "He understood my caution, and he even understood the questioning he got from my friends when he visited me in New Mexico. He was so open and natural about it. Even my most skeptical friends relaxed and wished us well on the cruise we were planning for our next step." The cruise included a discussion of marriage, and Patty is now planning a move to Maryland within the next year.

THE NET REALITY

For many mature women, online dating may seem to go against the grain of the advice we all once received about playing hard to get. Relationship experts in the past warned women to appear detached, to move with the stealth of a GI in camouflage bellying under barbed wire behind enemy lines. "Helpful" books and articles insisted that to show a man that we need him would put us in his rearview mirror, while remaining aloof would put us in his crosshairs. Yet posting a personal ad online feels like screaming, "I'm dying for some guy to let me smother him with my need for romance!" In reality, the men on that site wouldn't be there if they wanted a woman who was too coy to advertise what she wants. Don't sweat being direct.

Other women worry about the amount of time it will take to select, contact, and respond to men who may or may not turn out to be possible matches. But, if you are organized and clear about what you want and expressing who you are in your online ad, these problems can be minimized.

Lana's Avalanche of Responses

When we met Lana, who had posted a profile on three senior sites just two weeks earlier, she exclaimed, "It's raining frogs!" She was overwhelmed by the process of weeding out the "nos" from the "possibles," and when she spoke on the phone with one or another of her "possibles," she often mixed

A Formula for Cybersearchers

In his book *I Can't Believe I'm Buying This Book: A Commonsense Guide to Internet Dating*, Evan Marc Katz suggests that creativity, patience, and resilience are the three keys to success. Creativity is required when writing a profile and exchanging emails, patience enables you to wait until you find the right guy, and resilience enables you to get past disappointments and rejection.

up what she knew of them. She asked Tom, the bookworm, about his rock climbing and Jeff, the avid sailor, about his hike on the Appalachian Trail. She needed a better system, and she created one. She prints out the men's profiles and then files them in folders labeled, "Always a frog," "Might morph someday," and "Sounds princely." She adds notes to the folders as she interacts with her prospects, and she reshuffles the profiles among folders as potential royals disappoint or as frogs reinvent themselves.

The women who enjoy online dating and are successful at it approach it with wit and intelligence. They embrace the attitude that the experience can be an interesting and fun diversion even if they don't succeed in discovering the perfect man. With that outlook, the endeavor really can be fun, and you may meet some intriguing guys.

Tips for Increased Success

Be insightful about sites. Look at several web sites and try their free demonstration searches before you pay to belong. Sign up for a short-term membership at first and be prepared to switch sites if necessary. Understand the variables: sites may or may not charge for response emails, they may or may not offer private chat or instant messaging options, they may allow few or many profile essay changes, and they vary in their monthly charges and renewal fees.

Most of what you do to introduce yourself online is commonsensical. You already know things like you shouldn't adopt an overly cutesy screen name or fib when writing your profile. You can easily figure out that you should include a photo that makes you look radiantly happy and somewhat younger than your years. And you can quickly pick up some pointers on profile writing by reading the profiles of others and noting what sounds good to you and why. Write a profile that is specific about you and your interests, shows optimism and humor, depicts the real you, and indicates a desire to share what is already good about your life.

Activate your radar. A beautiful advantage of being over fifty is an increased ability to spot and steer away from anyone who just doesn't seem right. The Internet, like most other places where you can meet interesting men, can turn up some fibbers, losers, and con artists. Stay alert and check out the veracity of his claims at each step along the way.

Do not overanalyze the first face-to-face meeting. Plan to keep it short, perhaps meeting at a café for coffee. A good rule of thumb: For every hour it took you to prepare to look fabulous for that first meeting, spend only half an hour at the actual meeting. You can always follow up later, if you decide there is a later.

～

I learned about the amazing possibilities of
Internet dating among seniors the hard way. Well before we
divorced, I discovered my fifty-six-year-old husband had profiles
on two sites. Two weeks after our divorce, he married one of
the four ladies he had seriously dated after meeting online.
My kids tell me they seem very happy together.

—TERRY, 62, ADVERTISING EXECUTIVE

～

Now You See Him, Now You ... What?

Whether you are on the phone, facing a stranger in person, or getting reacquainted with an old friend, coming up with an opening line always seems like a big deal. How do you get his attention? How do you get the ball rolling?

Now that you are over fifty, your methods of getting noticed by a stranger should have changed dramatically since the cons you used thirty years ago or more. You don't stare blankly, drop a book in his path, or accidentally bump his elbow. You don't wiggle a hip, lift a shoulder, or lean over to provide a cleavage view. At your age, you get to do what comes naturally with someone you want to meet. First, you catch his eye and say "Hi" (or, if you're from the South, you say "Hey" to mean the same thing). Then, you remark on something relevant to both of you:

"Stunning exhibit, isn't it?"

"What perfect weather for biking."

"Your dog seems so well behaved."

Even better, you might ask a question:

"Did Dr. Jones say we have no class on Columbus Day?"

"How did you train your dog to heel so well?"

"Do you know where they keep the travel books?"

He can take it from there, or he can duck the whole encounter. You have nothing to lose. If he does take the bait and a conversation ensues, the same rules apply now that applied years ago:

❦ Look him in the eye.

❦ Smile, smile, smile.

❦ Listen, prompt him to continue, and listen some more.

The listening part is important not only for early encounters, but also for established friendships and romances moving well along. They all love to feel that they have enthralled you. The more you listen, the more they open up.

Of course, when you are not listening, you are talking. However, keep in mind that most men have their limits concerning women talking. Katherine learned that when one very nice man labeled her "the mouth of the South."

Connie, a sixty-three-year-old massage therapist, told us, "I have the best job in the world for capturing a man's interest. My whole job is to listen and make them feel good. I may be a total stranger, but, oh boy, do they open up to me. If I do much talking, I'm not doing my job, because they don't come to a massage therapist to hear about her life. It is amazing, at my age, how much I am still learning about men by listening to them. I don't actually date clients, but many have become good friends, and some have introduced me to their friends."

Your options for finding the men you can befriend, or bed, or wed have never been greater, and your opportunities have never been better. As long as you are willing to think strategically and act deliberately, you will eventually find them or him. He may be at a place that you frequent. Or, finding him may necessitate greater outreach—through friends, groups, reunions, holiday greetings, or the Internet. Try it all: volume is your best friend, and there is no overkill in this pursuit. Check out every possibility and embrace every new opportunity.

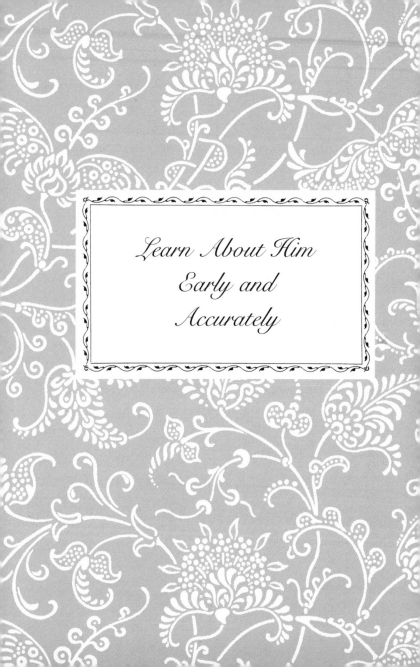

*Learn About Him
Early and
Accurately*

5

FOR FUN OR FOREVER?
A MATCH OR A MAYBE?

*T*HANKFULLY, YOU HAVE DISCOVERED there really are still guys out there who can be fun buddies, brief flings, or significant others—depending on your own preferences. You've managed to capture the attention of one or more of them. Maybe some romantic chemistry was sparked after a single lunch together, or maybe you launched a friendship in the waiting room of your vet's office. Either way, you still have ahead of you the tough sorting work that begins when you start asking questions like, "Am I nuts to be nuts about him so soon?" "If he is everything I never wanted, why do I feel such chemistry with him?" "He seems like a great pal for support and laughs, so does it matter that I have no romantic interest in him?"

Sandy went to lunch with a man she expected would continue to be a mere acquaintance. But their animated conversation covering many topics of common interest was so compelling that she fell in love while barely touching her Cobb salad. She floated back to her office, and an exciting new relationship took wing. Marina had known Rodney for a while and considered him a kind and good friend. They did a lot of fun things together as pals until gradually the sparks flew. Rose locked eyes with a stranger across a crowded cocktail party. He negotiated the room to her side, introduced himself, and suggested they leave and go somewhere quieter. She did and "zinged" right into an instant-attraction fling.

In the early stages of friendship or a budding romance, the actions you take should be aimed at addressing his compatibility with your needs. You need to determine how compatible you are as early as possible so you can decide whether to suspend your search in favor of the man of the moment or to move on to the men of the future. We call this the "go figure" stage—the shuffle, cut, and deal activity of deciding exactly how much time and energy you want to put into a guy who might or might not turn out to be what you're looking for.

Of course, you could entirely skip this step if you are one of those rare ladies who "just knows" at first sight and is happy ever after. But, unfortunately, those sightings are generally reserved for the miniseries that you watch when you are home alone with a cold, a box of aloe-infused tissues, and a

Psychologists who study romance have found that only about 10 to 15 percent of lasting relationships began as love at first sight on the part of either partner. Men make more snap judgments than women, sometimes deciding if they "click" with the lady they meet in less than a minute; but women need time to check things out.

deep pessimism about the chances that anyone interesting will set your cell phone vibrating. In reality, you are likely to have more questions than answers as you begin a relationship with the guy who might become your brotherly tennis partner, your short-term bed partner, or your special life partner.

Getting to Maybe

How do you figure out if he's a fling, a friend, or a forever after? Start by asking him lots of questions—preferably on the phone or in person, because too many men write only very short and unadorned emails. On the phone or in person, you can prompt him to elaborate with information that will tell you what he is really like. Ask questions such as those that follow to determine where he falls along a range of potential characteristics:

Intellectual Attributes: Is he a beautiful mind, a lover of learning, an atrophying brain?

> *Your question:* The Uptown is doing independent film screenings next week, and a few of them sound good. How about we go Friday night?

> *His answer:* I'm clueless about independent films, but I'm all for finding out. Let's do it.

> *His answer:* I was thinking we'd go to *War Martians Invade Earth* at the Superflix.

Physical Attributes: Is he an athlete, an active nonathlete, a couch potato, a couch?

> *Your question:* Everyone says Pilates is a super workout. Have you ever tried it?

> *His answer:* Never tried it; I'm stuck like a broken record on my morning routine of running and weight lifting.

> *His answer:* Pilates?

Emotional Attributes: Is he steady and calm, a duke of drama, emotionally challenged?

> *Your question:* My dog got out under the fence yesterday, and I was frantic until I found her; has that ever happened with your dog?

> *His answer:* Fido isn't that energetic, but if he did get out,

I'd be panicked that he might get lost or run over. You must have been beside yourself!

His answer: It happens. I stand at the back door with a cookie and call her. She'll show up either then or later. She loves cookies.

Social Style: Is he the life of the party, lively in spurts, glued to the hearth?

Your question: It's going to be a busy season of social whirl. Are you as overwhelmed with holiday invitations as I am?

His answer: Oh, yeah, I know what you mean. It's so hard to decide, but you just can't possibly make it to all of them.

His answer: I've received a few, but I generally prefer to stay at home anyway.

Communication Skills: Is he gifted with gab, allergic to small talk, a man of few words . . . and those few he uses rarely?

Your question: Did you see that gorgeous sunset last night?

His answer: Spectacular! I took some photos off the back deck. I was reading somewhere that the reds and oranges have something to do with the particulate matter in the air.

His answer: Yup.

Financial Acumen: Is he a man with a plan, a spendthrift, stingy?

Your question: Do you have to own investment real estate to diversify your investments?

His answer: Well, not necessarily. I've already got that because of how my company invests my retirement savings. So I'm enjoying my stock market investments with monthly dividends more because I can treat myself to little spurts of splurging.

His answer: That's what you hear; but then, if it skyrockets, what are you going to spend it on anyway?

Sense of Humor: Is he an entertainer, does he laugh with you, does he not get it?

Your question: What was your all time favorite *Saturday Night Live* skit?

His answer: Hands down, Steve Martin and ballet parking. I did that bit at a party once. No, maybe when Gilda did the toilet paper stuck to the shoe thing. But, wait, maybe Belushi as the rabbi . . .

His answer: My kids think all that stuff is hilarious.

Add other questions that may be important to you, but there is no need to get overly structured about the exercise. A lot of the items on this list will roll out naturally as you converse about the weather, your work, and the people you know in common. Clearly, there is no use in actually asking him if he has a sense of humor or an active mind. Instead, say something that would make most people laugh or question him about what books he is currently reading. You need only prompt (okay, prod) in a few areas.

If you know some of his friends, you can always gather additional information through them—but do so *very* subtly, so the friends don't know you are snooping. It's best to broadcast no more than a passing interest, because overly eager friends can be lethal to a budding relationship. You can also surf the Internet for any mentions of him, checking him out by name and through the web site of his employer. Your objective here is to get a complete picture that will help you sort out where he fits into your life and support your instinct that he is a guy you will want around for good fun or romance. The primary aim at this stage is to search for a sense of compatibility early on. We strongly advise you to address this promptly. The sooner you can discover which men are compatible and send the wrong ones packing the better! You don't have time to dwell on whether a particular man might fit into your life and, if he does, where in your life that might be. You want to figure this out early on. If your general conversation with him leaves you feeling puzzled about him, take a more direct approach. Katherine, for example, heard herself asking after just a few hours with a man with whom she felt a click, "So, do you think you could ever have a long-distance romance with someone 2,000 miles away?" His reply said it all: "That's the only kind

of relationship I could imagine having at this time in my life."
We're not suggesting that level of pushiness as a regular mode
of operation, but moving with due speed is crucial.

Elise's Too-Long Goodbye

*We spoke to Elise, a fifty-five-year-old divorced insurance
agent, about a relationship with a man that was incompat-
ible from the start, but that she ended only after two years
of effort. She recalls, "Paul was a good person—really
good. Hardworking, financially well-off, honest, smart,
funny, patient, unmarried, and great in bed. We had a long-
distance relationship, spending maybe forty or so days a year
together. I wanted those days to be special, with togetherness,
hand holding, and hugs. In between visits, I longed for phone
calls and emails that indicated he cared and missed me—
although I was not seeking a long-term commitment. He
wanted to fit me around his busy work schedule, emailed
me almost never, phoned only when he multitasked the call
during his commute, and left me alone a lot when I visited
him. He had little interest in celebrating holidays, surprising
me with silly gifts, or even giving much indication that he
cared about me. Although he seemed to thoroughly enjoy our
time together, he did nothing to make it longer or deeper. I
realized within a few months that he wanted a woman in his
life only in a superficial and occasional way—for things like*

foot massages and good cooking—but he was emotionally unable to have an actual relationship in his life, even a long-distance one with no commitment. I needed a more caring and supportive relationship. We talked about this, but Paul could not bring himself to be there for me. It took me way too long to close the door on that nonrelationship, because even though his behavior left me feeling hurt a lot, I truly enjoyed the small amount of interaction we did have. But it just wasn't what I needed or wanted for myself. If I'd been thinking more about what I needed in the first place, I could have avoided a lot of frustration."

Even if you realize that you're not compatible with someone and that you're not getting what you want, terminating a budding relationship can be difficult. Good and available men over fifty are not easy to find, and giving one up because he doesn't match your preferences can be wrenching. It generally happens only after we've wasted time trying to fit ourselves into his mold or trying to change him to fit ours. Better you should avoid that wrong relationship in the first place.

We hope there is a deserving woman out there who really wants a continuing series of superficial flings with a busy person, and we hope that she has now found Paul. The key is to find the person who can give you what you seek. Ask yourself these two questions: Does this relationship make me feel really good? Does this relationship get in my way of finding other, more fulfilling relationships? If you answer "no" to the first or "yes" to the second, you are wasting your time. Find a way out as soon as possible. Next time, don't even go there.

Remember: To err is human. To err on the side of keeping someone around when he doesn't meet your needs—whether as a caring pal or a committed partner—is a waste of your time. Don't be afraid of reactivating your search when you realize that a budding relationship won't work. We all know the woman who clings like lint to the first guy who shows an interest in her because she thinks it's either him or being alone. But soon being alone is looking pretty good To avoid this common trap, act quickly on your intuition, the information you have gathered, and your general sense of what can work for you at this time. If you have had your fill of short-term flings but the man you have met is clear that he isn't looking for a serious relationship, move on quickly. Likewise, if you prefer only noncommittal short-term fun at this point but Mr. Serious shows up, don't mislead him. Tell him you're only ready to be a good pal right now. Then gather your best female friends around you, plan a fun weekend, and discover that you aren't alone after all.

We encourage only two exceptions to the rule of determining the potential of a relationship before investing too much energy:

- Old guy pals who pass your way only occasionally and make you feel good without taking up too much time or energy

- Special-purpose guys who are your professional mentors, your pals for attending movies or wine tastings, your auto mechanics, your concerned and helpful neighbors

These men are fun and useful additions to your life who are only in your orbit on occasion and can be kept there without worries about their compatibility. They are different from the men you hope will stick around to chat after joining you on your power walk around the park or from the men who pop up in your thoughts at the oddest times of day. If you miss someone, wonder when you'll see him again, or think about him nearly every day, he has the makings of a great friend or a potential romance. Otherwise, he may be a drop-by pal or a special-purpose guy.

Which Is He?

You're interested. He's interested. You've been out a few times. But it's so difficult to tell where he fits into your life. Is he a fling, a friend, or a forever after? Here are some guidelines that may help you decide:

A *fling* or *frolic* is Mr. Fun Times. He calls once every other week or so. He always invites you to a great party, a fun rock concert, a professional sporting event, or even a weekend in the Bahamas. He is great to be with, and you always have a wonderful time. If you don't care about what he is doing or where he is in between his surprise phone calls, go for it. He plays the field, and he won't change. Why should he? He's having fun. So, you have fun too. Just don't start to care about him.

A male *friend* is not too different from your female friends. He is there for you as you are for him. You support each other, enjoy each other's company, and have fun together, but no sparks are flying.

A *forever after* may start out as a fling, a frolic, or a friend and grow into a solid relationship, or you may know instantly that he's a serious prospect. Your first instincts that he's a good match for you have been supported with the information you have learned over time. In Step 7, you will go through a checklist that will help you decide if your man is, indeed, a keeper.

Could He Be Just Right? Tricky Questions Answered

Questions about how to approach men as well as how to deal with early relationship issues are still with us at fifty-plus. And although these questions are relevant for both platonic buddies and romantic partners, they become trickier in situations headed toward romantic chemistry:

Question: He works in my company, we've always been warm friends at the office, and his wife just died after a long illness. What's my best approach?

Answer: The well-worn advice is still true: Be the first one there with a casserole. Attractive widowers typically move fast to the next relationship, so make sure the seven ladies lined up behind you don't stand a chance. For variety, however, we recommend you arrive with a spiral-cut ham or fully cooked beef tenderloin. Add sliced Swiss or cheddar cheese, jars of gourmet mustard and mayonnaise, and a head of lettuce. Men love big sandwiches. Additionally, include him when you are having friends of varying ages over for burgers and Monday night football. That way you are extending support with no specific agenda.

Question: I have had some great conversations with this very interesting single man who lives up the street, and we've even walked our dogs around the block together several times. But he's made no moves beyond that, so how can I get this thing going?

Answer: A fairly direct route is best in this case, because you need to find out if he is already committed elsewhere, overly busy, or just a very slow mover. Ask him some candid questions about his past and future. If you are still interested, ask him over for a drink.

Question: I can't believe it, but two men seem to be possible romantic interests right now. One I enjoy best for fun, laughter, and outdoorsy companionship, the other for romantic, physical attraction. How soon do I have to decide between them?

Answer: Why do you ever need to decide? Enjoy them both until one drifts off, morphs into "just a friend," or lets his flaws become more evident. (For us, physical attraction always eventually wins out.)

Question: We seem so compatible on many levels, although we have barely reached the romantic stage after about three months. Still, I get anxious when he says he'll be in touch and then lets thirteen days go by. Should I mention this to him?

Answer: Don't bother. He's a guy. This is what they do. Put up or move on, depending on your tolerance level for boorish, juvenile behavior. Emilie decided she wouldn't play this game and responded with "see ya!" Katherine confronted the man who acted this way, only to be told, "You're just being hypersensitive."

Question: I'd like to see how he is around my grown kids. How soon is too soon to invite him to a family get together?

Answer: The later the better. Your kids are grown and out of the house, so your only real concern is how he is around you.

Question: He seems the nearly perfect pal who could join me in lots of interesting social activities. So why does it worry me that his ninety-year-old mother lives with him?

Answer: It worries us, too. Unless she has a separate guest house on the property and is lively enough to care for herself, he may be a poor relative living off her pension.

Question: I'm very attracted to him, but he's still got a lot of baggage from his former marriage. But that ended eight years ago, so what gives?

Answer: Some guys hang onto the baggage because they get strokes for the "wounded bird" act. It's an emotional con, and he's not worth your further consideration.

Question: I love being with him, and he seems to love being with me, but that is almost never, because he's so busy with his demanding work and numerous personal commitments. Should I push him on this?

Answer: Oh, the excuses we've heard! Notice how he makes time for his old golfing buddies, his lawyer, his mother? Ask him very directly about the lack of time spent with you and pay attention to the answer. He may never want to make time for a partner. If you like lots of alone time, that will work. Otherwise, move on.

Question: He's got a boyish charm that I love, but he holds way back when it comes to doing the little things—no unexpected phone calls just to say hi, no putting on music that he knows I really like, no small compliments about how I look. Do I say anything about this?

Answer: Not yet, unless his lax behavior also includes leaving the toilet seat up. Give him another chance by doing (and saying) lots of nice things to see if he'll get the idea and reciprocate.

Special Moves for Special Types

Although it is difficult to accurately plumb the psyche of any man just because he has certain characteristics, we can make some broad generalizations about those men who fall into a few categories that merit special handling. Widowers and bachelors, for example, have particular traits that you need to keep in mind. The same is true of much younger and older men and recently divorced men. That's not to say that men who fall in these categories can't be a real possibility for fun or romance, but it does help to arm yourself with an awareness that you may need to approach them differently than others.

The Wiley Widower

He's got the need to grieve, a closet full of baggage, and a cute vulnerability. However, in order to become whole again, he needs to receive far more than he can give, making him a dubious prospect for perhaps a year or more after the death of his wife. The catch-22? His neediness at the early widower stage prompts him to gravitate to new women very quickly. If you don't move into his orbit, someone else will. But if you get involved with him you may find yourself getting the short end of the stick.

Typically, a widower needs to work through the gamut of grief, guilt, and perhaps anger after the death of his wife. He is lonely; you are there to keep him company. He is uncomfortable in his new role as homemaker and social secretary and dislikes filling all the other roles once filled by his wife; you are there to soothe his discomfort. He is stymied about the etiquette of dealing with people who want to comfort and assist; you are there to support and advise. If you can deal with these realities, at least for a while, by all means be there, but don't expect a great deal in return too soon.

- ❧ **Where to find him:** At his daughter's home. In church. At his office. In the deli section of the supermarket. On his front stoop picking up the three-bean salad left by your competition.

- ❧ **How to spot him:** He is wearing mismatched socks. He frowns a lot, looking more puzzled than stern. He looks tired but sweet with his bedroom eyes. His downward cast has an appealing sadness.

- ❧ **What to know about him:** He needs time. He needs space. He needs a woman.

Susan's Widower

When Bill, age seventy-four, lost his wife of more than forty years to cancer, he soldiered on alone for eight days before he phoned an old high school friend, Susan, age seventy-three. He hadn't kept in touch with Susan, but he had always felt a chemistry when they unexpectedly met about every five years. He knew she was living in a town about sixty miles away and was now single after two marriages that ended in divorce and another two that ended in widowhood. Bill's opening remark to Susan was, "I just can't do this alone. Can you come visit?" She arrived almost immediately and never left. With the help of some remarkable chemistry, as well as the patience she had developed through her experiences with four husbands, she nudged Bill through difficult months and then married him. Susan, candid and irreverent, later told us, "At my age, I understand men all too well, so my expectations are limited. I didn't need him to do a lot for me, other than let me enjoy his company. He needed me much worse, especially at first, so it worked out incredibly well for us. I've decorated his new condominium and kept him in touch with his three grown children, grandchildren, and friends. I plan our travel and little social occasions. Basically, I just create a buffer between him and his temptation to live life as a curmudgeon."

THE BALDING BACHELOR

His fear of commitment has stood him in such good stead for so long that you almost have to admire him. Then you notice his lack of sensitivity to your needs. He only responds when and how he wants to respond—and that includes to everything from your emails to your hugs and kisses. Bachelors are typically accustomed to giving less than they receive. Except possibly to their mothers. Why would they be any other way after all those years alone? Well, not exactly alone; many, if not most, have had numerous relationships. With every relationship, it has gotten easier and easier to avoid compromise, to continue to look for that perfect woman who is never difficult, never dissatisfied. The idea of working on a relationship with a woman is typically foreign to an older man who has never been married. Ever hopeful, he is more likely to opt for a new—this time perfect—woman. This cycle tends to repeat itself over and over again, and significant relationships continue to elude the life-long bachelor, who quickly gives up on interactions that are not trouble-free.

The statistics indicate that bachelors almost never marry if they haven't tied the knot by age fifty. On the other hand, many commitment-phobic women, as well as women looking for friends or transitional relationships, may find exactly what they seek in a confirmed bachelor—a guy who lets you relax and enjoy without confronting the "Where do we go from here?" discussion. As platonic friends or as sexual partners, bachelors can be perfect for women who don't want to deal with emotional entanglement. It is important, however, to be very, *very* clear about what you are looking for, because you will *not* change the habits that keep him comfortable and single. Attempts to get him to vary his patterns are about as successful as eliminating cellulite by applying creams. Just go with the flow, get what you need, and be ready to exit.

～

I was twice divorced; he had always been single.
I was romantic and sensitive; he was pragmatic and insensitive.
I was a talkative social type; he was a quiet workaholic.
Great chemistry kept us together for two years. Then I moved
on so I could search for a real relationship.

—MARION, 56, TEACHER

～

❧ **Where to find him:** Puttering around in his garage or garden. At work. At his mother's house. At an antiques store. At an electronics store.

❧ **How to spot him:** He is the one on his mother's arm at a family funeral. On the weekend, he is wearing khakis— perhaps jeans. He has good electronic equipment but only so-so clothes and home furnishings.

❧ **What to know about him:** He is self-sufficient and rarely lonely. He is not very sensitive to your emotional needs, but he will go the extra mile to help on impersonal tasks. He is a bit fussy but even-tempered. He is quiet, but very firm in his convictions. He loves his cat.

THE DIVORCED DERVISH

He's finally having a good time now that his past wife and past life are out of the picture. Is his good time with you just that? Or can it be something deeper? The divorced man may feel a victim or victorious—depending on his circumstances, the amount of time passed, and his general attitude. Assume that a newly divorced man is on the rebound, suffering sadness and guilt. This does not lead to savvy decision making. Or, he may feel hurt, puzzled, and bruised. This also does not readily guide him to the next perfect relationship.

Give him time. He will get over it. Better yet, don't even meet him until he is already over it. In other words, when your friends tell you about Jim, their neighbor who needs to meet a wonderful new lady now that his divorce became final last week, be skeptical. How long was he separated? Are his wounds still raw? Is he simply ready to scratch an itch? Or, was he perhaps psychologically divorced well before his actual separation and divorce? If so, he might be that rare recently divorced individual who is not actually on the rebound. And if that's the case, he might select the right woman. If not, he will still select a woman, but he'll probably quickly decide she isn't quite right. Like we said, this is murky water that deserves your extreme caution. Still, we have to say that even the recently divorced man is not necessarily a hopeless case for the woman who is realistic about the long-term possibilities.

- **Where to find him:** Frequenting health clubs and upscale bars. Joining friends at good restaurants. Attending national sports events.

- **How to spot him:** He is slightly rumpled or deliberately underdressed. He wears black shirts under a khaki jacket. He is tired but tanned, and he smiles a lot.

- **What to know about him:** He is eager but wary and rarely relaxed. He is physically affectionate and knows how to please a woman. He may or may not be a talker; if so, he is likely to talk mostly about himself.

THE YOUNGER HUNK

He's got the moves that boost your ego and liven your libido. Enjoy! What is not to like about a guy who is ten or more years your junior and adores you? He makes you feel younger, and he teaches you things—from young lingo to young music to young moves for romance and pleasure. The mere knowledge that someone younger is interested in you becomes the headwaters of your fountain of youth. You simply cannot act your age when you know you are attractive to a younger man. Instead, you become lighthearted. You smile more and fret less.

You may begin to worry about how long this can last. Does he really understand that at fifty-plus you're not a girl anymore? Can you manage to hide those AARP newsletters and senior citizen discount coupons? What happens ten or twenty years from now, when he's thinking about a prescription for erectile dysfunction and you're thinking there is no prescription for loss of bladder control? Many younger men date older women briefly as experiments, but then quickly retreat. Others seek financial security, mothering, or professional contacts.

Emilie advises to avoid overanalyzing his motives. As she found out, he may very well be a caring and wonderful guy who has found dozens of reasons to be with you that have nothing to do with your age. So enjoy your good fortune. If it changes ten years from now, you will still have had ten wonderful years.

- **Where to find him:** At live music venues: jazz clubs, cowboy bars, concerts. Picking up his kids from middle school. On the ski slopes, the beach, or mountain bike trails.

- **How to spot him:** He is all smiles, lively, and alert. He wears his clothes so naturally that you don't notice what he's wearing. He has good hair, but not necessarily a good haircut. He is among friends.

- **What to know about him:** He really likes women, especially women with the benefit of experience. He likes the ability of older women to be unpretentious and direct, and he hopes they stay that way. He has a very good sense of humor.

THE OLD FART

He is a dear old fellow, and he's a sweetheart when he wants to be. But is he with you because of your charms or because of your nursing skills? He may be the man of your dreams, the one who makes you feel wanted, needed, cared for, and complete. Or, he may be the one who keeps you very busy and very tied down for the next ten or twenty years. The unpredictability of his health issues makes it impossible to know much about what your future with a man in his seventies or eighties will look like. You may feel fulfilled in the Florence Nightingale role . . . but you might not. You could be pushing a wheelchair for many years to come. Is that really for you?

Reflect and imagine the possible futures before you get very far with a much older man. Think about your needs, your energy level, and your desire for an active life. And, perhaps most importantly, think about your financial situation. We know women who have depleted their own retirement funds in order to care for an older mate. Other women, however, have been granted his higher Social Security payments. In the meantime, however, they have had warm and fulfilling relationships. The bottom line: Think about the future and get a professional opinion from a financial advisor before you jump in.

- **Where to find him:** At the symphony and on the golf course. At book clubs and in libraries. At his next door neighbor's holiday brunch.

- **How to spot him:** He is silver or bald and a bit stooped. He wears clothes that seem a size or two too big for him. He lives in a small condominium or a large house with an unkempt yard.

- **What to know about him:** His health and his family come first. His grandchildren really matter. His tennis game may surprise you, and Viagra works for him. He loves the country club life.

THE AGING ATTORNEY OR SILVER SURGEON

He is educated, intelligent, interesting, wealthy, and retired. He's smart enough to know what women want. He belongs to a country club, plays golf and tennis, and likely has a second home somewhere. He likes to travel, especially with a companion—you.

While the situation is perfect, he may or may not be. Men in high-powered professions are accustomed to being in charge and being catered to. Outside the professional setting, they rarely take care of others. Instead, they are likely to be in the habit of issuing orders and receiving immediate compliance. Their professional success stems from the dedication and hard work they demand of themselves and others. So, while he may be intriguing and exciting, he may also be a controlling pain in the butt; he may demand devotion, agreement, and slavish attention in return for the affluent lifestyle he can provide. This type of man can work well for women who value the good material life and are not in the position to achieve it on their own and who also require minimal emotional support. If that does not describe you, find a caring retired carpenter or teacher who will smother you with love.

- ❧ **Where to find him:** Sunday brunch at the country club. The pro shop. The putting green or driving range. Charity functions—especially those related to legal aid or diseases.

- ❧ **How to spot him:** He is smartly, conservatively, and expensively dressed. He experiments with pink shirts and with patterned pants. He carries himself with authority and sports a good haircut and a recent manicure.

- ❧ **What to know about him:** He is charming, well read, well traveled, and a good escort. He may be self-centered and narcissistic. He has plenty of interesting male associates, but is not close to any of them. He gives lovely gifts, although they rarely relate especially to your interests.

Now It's Your Turn . . .

Most of the foregoing is about *your* response to *him*. What about the things you do to provoke (yes, absolutely provoke) his response? After all, you want to be in control of finding him, and keeping him, if you choose. You don't want him to jump overboard while you're still considering the matter.

One thing we learned from several of Katherine's Southern girlfriends is the Magnolia Principle. It's that way that Southern ladies have of bringing men to their knees that can seem pretty silly to a Yankee girl; but, on Yankee men and others from points south, east, and west, *it works*. It works because it is oh-so-girly, which makes a guy feel oh-so-manly, which is exactly what a guy wants to feel most of all. But by definition, he can only feel manly in the context of girly. A Southern lady working the Magnolia Principle gets to hand Mr. Manly his ego on a platter.

Lucy Ellen's Magnolia Strategy

Our sixty-two-year-old girly friend Lucy Ellen from Oxford, Mississippi, told us how she averted an early near-breakup with the man she has now been with for three years: "I suspected he was going to tell me in some kind of sideways fashion that we were cooling off after just two or three months. So, when he came over, I had him sit on the front porch swing with me and take off his shoes. I gave him a glass of sweet tea, and I was dressed in a frilly silk dress with flowers around the hemline. I asked him all about his day, his work, his golf weekend coming up; and I just kept urging his answers on with lots of giggling at little things he said, gazing intently and nodding. He seemed pleased as punch that I was so enthralled.

Only once in almost two hours did he start to come to the point with, 'You know, you and I . . .' I just cut him off immediately by shrugging my shoulders and telling him, 'Oh, it's such a lovely evening, let's don't fuss about anything that would spoil it.' He sort of forgot all about the cooling off."

KEY ELEMENTS OF THE MAGNOLIA PRINCIPLE

This list describes the full-court girly push. You can be selective, adapt it to your own style, and still go a long, long way.

Eyelashes: Big (four layers of mascara) and ready to bat.

Gazes: Alternately downward and wide into his eyes.

Questions: All about him. Short statements about you only when asked.

Intent listening: With nodding, murmuring, giggles.

Mouth: Always smiling, often laughing, showing very white teeth.

Reactions: Blush, bat eyes, widen eyes, small catch of breath, keep smiling.

Gestures: Your hand moving lightly across your own throat or shoulders.

Touch: Your hand slightly tapping his knee or shoulder from time to time.

Dress: Feminine to the nines. Fabrics that move, floral prints, age-appropriate ruffles, lace, ribbon. Under that, silky little things.

Shoes: Lots of thin straps.

Nails: Perfectly manicured fingers and toes. Pale pink translucent polish.

Scent: Yes, if it is a waft of magnolia, crape myrtle, or gardenia softened with a bit of lemon or spice.

Whether we like it or not, girly can be very effective. Of course, we appreciate that most of us spent years fighting the good feminist battle in our homes and our workplaces. But when your new relationship has you thinking romance, you've got to look it, breathe it, show it. No, you do *not* need to change from your level-headed, take-charge, intelligent self to a gushy lump of uncertainty. The Magnolia Principle asks you to adjust the outer shell, not the inner you. Your professional clothing might consist of fabulous Armani suits, but Ralph Lauren is right about the romance of all things white and filmy.

The unexpected advantage of this approach is that it puts you in charge; he is putty. It also has a way of making you feel good about yourself. Believe us, it takes almost no time at all to get over the worry that you could be selling out on your feminist sisters when a man is falling all over you. You'll feel great about yourself and your promising future.

A suggestion from Emilie, whose feminist outlook won't allow her to employ the Magnolia Principle: at least ask him for help with everything you need help doing.

A FEW GOOD IDEAS HELP ATTRACT A FEW GOOD MEN

Long lists of dos and don'ts about handling a budding relationship are for ladies who stopped thinking for themselves when June Cleaver was still an American icon. For you, our savvy friend, a few good ideas will suffice as reminders that can be adapted to his particular qualities and foibles:

- **Pay attention.** Ask questions and be raptly attentive. Keep those queries impersonal at first—about his dog, his work, the books he reads. Then move on ever so carefully to his childhood, his family, his children, and his ex-wife.

- **Tell him about you—with your mouth shut.** Your actions will speak plenty. You are lovely, interested, lighthearted, and warm. Show, don't tell—at least to a greater extent than you do in other circumstances.

- **Be gracious.** If he gives you his favorite book, read it. If he gives you a meat thermometer, use it. If he gives you a T-shirt, wear it. Thank him verbally and with your actions.

- **Need his help.** Ask for his advice: "Who is your accountant?" "Should I be using synthetic oil?" Ask for his expertise and knowledge: "What does it mean when my car wobbles at high speeds?" "When is the best time to train my hydrangea?" Ask for his help: "Can you give me a hand with installing this new computer graphic program?"

- ❧ **Compliment him a lot.** You can't do this too often. Tell him how much you like his car, his dog, his yard, his tennis game, his clothes. After he helps you, tell him his assistance was invaluable.

- ❧ **Call him, email him, invite him—with a purpose.** Wait until you have a reason to contact him, even if you have to invent one. Don't call "just to say hi" or "just to see how you are doing," unless you've mutually agreed the relationship is only a friendship, or it's a high-level romance. Otherwise, make contact when you need to ask him something, return something of his, or solicit his advice.

- ❧ **Be direct, but not pushy.** There is nothing wrong with wanting a man in your life. There is also nothing wrong with him knowing that. But be subtle, not forward, about letting him know. It's not that men scare away easily; it's just that they are sometimes intimidated by overly direct women.

To recap: Now you should be taking action to determine if he is right for the relationship you want. Acquiring a little practical knowledge related to the psychology of his particular situation is always a good idea. So is simply being with him, asking him questions, listening to him, and getting to understand him in light of what you know you need and want.

Get Ready for Intimacy—
the Fun and Facts
of Mature Sex

6

BETTER SEX NOW THAN EVER

OKAY, YOU GOT UP, YOU GOT OUT, and you decided to soar. In fact, you've identified at least one potential partner, and you're considering plummeting into bed with him. But, a little voice inside you is saying, "I'm too old. I'm too fat. I'm too skinny. I've got scars. This is silly. What am I thinking?"

Well, nix those negatives. Yes, sex with a new partner sometimes strikes you as inappropriate at this time of life as a spring break trip to Fort Lauderdale, but it is also a warm and fun adventure. So you have a few bulges or scars from babies, surgery, or trauma. Who cares? You're a grown-up. You've been living life, not measuring it out in coffee spoons like T. S. Eliot's J. Alfred Prufrock. And, you've made the decision to go on living with gusto. Sex is a great part of living, and you are about to take the plunge. Pat yourself on the back, rev up your endorphins, and get going. You will only feel foolish for a little while, anyway. Once you begin to purr along with foreplay those lovely brain chemicals take over, and you forget about everything else except the moment you are in. Promise!

If you need a more practical justification to get your motor revving, just keep telling yourself that sex is a health issue. It is essential to your well-being, just like keeping your cholesterol down, flossing your teeth, and eating your vegetables. Some commonly known health benefits of sex are:

- Calories burned—lots more fun than the treadmill

- Better heart health—it's a great cardio workout

- Improved immune system—and more fun than eating your vegetables

- Reduced stress—results in a tired and happy body and mind

- Increased sense of well-being—better than Prozac

- Glowing skin—gets the blood flowing

- Reduced vaginal dryness—using it prevents losing it

None of Us Are Teenagers

Let's talk about body image. What is yours? Not good, huh? Welcome to 90 percent of the middle-aged world—both men and women. None of us are eighteen, nor do we really want to be, even if the youth-obsessed entertainment industry and advertisers have taught us that we should look like anorexic models and should feel guilty if we don't. We are not "perfect ten" movie stars. And movie stars are not "perfect tens" either in real life. Have you ever seen candid photos of these gorgeous icons? They have cellulite, zits, scars, bulging stomachs, and protruding bones. They are real people too! Movie makers and advertisers are all in the illusion business, and we all buy into it.

Now look around you. Look at couples about your age who appear to be happy. You may see them walking down the street, shopping, eating dinner, or sitting in church. Are they all gorgeous? Look at couples you know who found each other later in life. Are they perfect? All these people are together, and most of them are having good sex with bodies plagued by lumps and creases. So, you're not perfect. And any man who interests you won't be perfect either. And he is just as worried as you are about the whole getting naked thing.

～⌒つ

Jack and I were becoming close, and I didn't know how to tell him about my mastectomy. When I'd had the surgery twenty years ago I had skipped reconstruction to get home to my three young children and my husband said he loved me just the way I was. I'd been widowed a number of years and hadn't yet had to address the issue of my single boob. Finally, I worked up

The men with good values—the decent and kind men, the men you want in your life because you are worthy of having good people around you—will not care about your love handles, your stretch marks, your flat chest, or your hysterectomy scar. (In fact, they might like that one.) Emilie's left leg was badly injured in the same incident that killed her husband. Several operations later she had a muscle indentation and a large scar from her hip almost to her knee. It wasn't a pretty sight. Although insurance would have covered plastic surgery, Emilie was tired of doctors by then and decided to just live with her leg the way it was.

Several years later, vacationing in Cancun with a girlfriend, Emilie could not avoid appearing in a bathing suit. After a lengthy conversation with herself, she decided that anyone who considered her leg unsightly didn't have to look at it. Cooling off in the pool while reading her book, she met a man who was also vacationing with a friend. The two sets of vacationing friends got together a couple of evenings for dinner and dancing, making the vacation more fun for all. Everyone's apparent acceptance of her scarred leg made Emilie more confident later when casually dating a fun former acquaintance. Fortified by her new *who cares?* attitude, as well as a couple glasses of wine, she showed her scar when he asked to see it. His response was, "Oh, that's no big deal." And, for Emilie, it never was again.

Take a look at that man who has attracted your interest. Is he a perfect specimen? Chances are he isn't. Of course, his physical appearance attracts you, but does it have to compete favorably with a lifeguard in Santa Monica? Certainly not. Why does he interest you? You are looking at a total package: a nice face, an interesting intellect, a display of warmth and joy. He is probably as worried as you about his body, so concentrate on making him feel confident about himself. This will take your mind off of yourself and your insecurities. A positive mental attitude, a gleam in your eye, a smile on your face, and a spring in your step are all much more attractive and valuable than an eighteen-year-old's body.

Refresher Course Needed?

It's a little scary dipping back into sexual waters after a long hiatus or many years with one partner with whom sex was as comfortable as your old moth-eaten slippers. You think you've forgotten all that you once knew, or perhaps you realize that there are things you never did know. You are a college freshman who just passed Missionary Position 101, and there are people out there with Ph.D.s in sex. How do you catch up? Easy. Take a refresher course.

Unlike during the days of your adolescence, when your limited information came from searching out the good parts in your parents' copy of *Peyton Place,* today information about sex is everywhere. You can't avoid it. Take a look at the magazines in the grocery store checkout line. Which ones jump out at you with articles about sex advertised in bold print? *Cosmopolitan? Glamour?* Buy them. Even those directed to the younger generation offer some good ideas for new and inventive pleasuring in bed. We recently spotted article titles like: "Ten Things You Don't Know about Sex but Should," "How to Blow His Mind in Bed," "Seven Strange Ideas Guys Have about Sex," and "The Kiss Men Crave the Most." Of course, if you are like Emilie, you will purchase this reading material at a grocery store in the next town where none of the checkout clerks knows you. But, if you are like Katherine, you will save money by quickly reading the articles while standing in the checkout line without worrying about who sees you.

Magazine articles, however, no matter how interesting, do not give you comprehensive information. Some books do. There are many good ones on mature sex, some researched and written by doctors, which will answer every question you have as well as some that have never even occurred to you. Check out the shelves in the "Health" section at your favorite bookstore or visit your local library. When you ask the librarian to point you toward the right area, you won't be the first person who has asked for books on sex, and the librarian won't remember you two minutes later anyway. Or use the library's computer card catalog, using the keywords "sex" and "sexual." You don't need to memorize everything you read for use later. You simply need to build your confidence by getting some ideas of things that will work for you. Once you are actually in the heat of the moment with someone, your instincts will take over, and you will have a fun, rousing, and mutually fulfilling experience.

The following is a recap of some of the resources you can rely on when constructing your refresher course:

- **Magazines** (interesting, but not comprehensive)

- **Books** (usually comprehensive, and there are a variety to select from)

- **Friends** (helpful for building your confidence, but not always accurate)

- **Television** (try *Sex Talk* on the Oxygen Channel—Dr. Sue Johanson is informative, fun, and reassuring)

- **DVDs** (rent *Sex and the City* or *Same Time Next Year*)

- **Movies** (try watching cutting-edge sexy movies, but avoid porn)

- **Your doctor** (you should see him or her anyway)

Medical Issues

When was your last gynecological checkup? Your doctor is your best resource for all of your questions about your physical condition, health and disease issues, and any other medical concerns. So schedule an appointment with your gynecologist or your primary care doctor today. Ask questions. Your doctors will be delighted you are living a full life and will only be too glad to talk with you about good sexual health in the new millennium. Write down all of your questions and take them with you when you see the doctor. If you want to do a little research first on your own, visit the library or bookstore or search the web. Some excellent web sites that give basic medical information include the Mayo Clinic at Mayohealth.org, the National Institutes of Health at www.nih.gov, Web MD at Webmd.com, and Healthfinder.gov. By doing a little bit of research first, you can get clear on the questions you want to ask your doctor and make sure your appointment time is well spent.

Part of your chat with your doctor should cover the subject of HIV, HIV testing, sexually transmitted infections, and the use of condoms. For many people condoms are not an issue because for them "sex" consists of something other than sexual intercourse, such as lots of cuddling and stroking or hand holding. If this is what brings you and your partner a sense of satisfaction and comfort, this is perfect for you. However, if you do plan to have sexual intercourse, ask your doctor to help you assess your risk factors for HIV and other sexually transmitted infections. Chances are your response will not be as extreme as that of Charlene, an attorney in Atlanta whose reaction was, "Condoms! Eeeek! I haven't seen one of those since I was sixteen years old and in the back of Joe Bob's 1968 Chevy. No way!" Nor will you resort to the extreme caution exercised by Denise, a retired systems analyst in Tampa, Florida, who not only carried with her and used condoms without fail, but also insisted that every possible partner, even those over seventy, have a current HIV test. She said, "I don't care who they are, or how important they are, or how snooty a country club they belong to. We are all at risk."

When Ann's thirty-something daughter Sarah realized that her mother's relationship with Dennis had become intimate, the conversation went like this:

Sarah: "Mother, you and Dennis are using condoms, aren't you?"

Ann: "No."

Sarah: "Mother! That's terrible! You could get AIDS or other diseases like gonorrhea or herpes! You absolutely have to use condoms."

Ann: "Sarah, I am a widow, and I only ever slept with your father. Dennis has been divorced for two years and only ever slept with his wife. We do not need to use condoms."

Sarah dragged me to this store on Clark Street called Condomania.
What a place! There were condoms with flags on them, stars, all
kinds of designs and flavors and sizes! After I got over my surprise,
it got to be pretty funny. But I didn't buy any.

—ANN, 61, RETIRED ANTHROPOLOGIST

If you decide condoms are a necessity, learn how to put them on your partner. This may take some persistence. They require unwrapping, unrolling, pinching the space at the tip, and avoiding punctures, so keep at it if it seems puzzling at first. Practice on a carrot or a zucchini—maybe even a banana. You should be so lucky! The point is to have fun, relax, and enjoy your sex life.

Setting the Sexy Scene

Now that you've worked on your confidence and made a commitment to fun and healthy sex, what next? Go shopping—for your bedroom, for your bathroom, and for yourself!

If there is even the slightest possibility that your sexual life is going to play out in your bedroom, walk in there right now and take stock. How old is that mattress? Those pillows? Those sheets? Give your bedroom a makeover. Replace an old, too-firm mattress with a new pillow-top mattress. If that's not in your budget, buy a thick pillow-top mattress cover.

There are plenty of discount stores and web sites where new bedding can be bought for reasonable prices. Type the words "bed linens" into a search engine, and a variety of sites will pop up. Check out ads and hit the sales at your local discount and department stores. Replace your pillows unless you bought them within the last three years. Most people keep their pillows, which accumulate germs and dust mites, for much too long. Unless you are determined to have premium down-filled pillows, they are not expensive to replace. After stumbling on a sale at a department store Emilie stockpiled a bunch of pillows of various degrees of firmness so she would be prepared for whatever the gentleman in question preferred. Since she'd only paid five dollars for each pillow, she could just throw them out with the gentleman's cooties when a particular relationship faded away. Luckily, she only lost a couple of pillows before she settled in with her current significant other—a man who sleeps with no pillow at all!

Now that you've freshened your mattress and replaced your pillows, it's time to evaluate your bedding. Are there any rips or stains? How long has your dog or cat been sleeping on the bed? Wash or dry clean everything. If the stains won't come out, replace the bedding. If you have tears that can't be hidden by tucking them under the bed, put those items on a shelf for use in emergencies. Even if you don't absolutely need a new blanket or bed cover, consider purchasing new ones anyway, to spruce up the bedroom. An absolute "must," however, is purchasing at least one new set of sheets and pillowcases, which will symbolize your fresh start in this new phase of life. Do *not* buy sheets in solid dark colors. Men buy those for their own beds and wash them infrequently. Wash the sheets several times after you buy them, and iron at least the top third of the top sheet as well as the pillow cases. A clean, fresh-smelling bed will feel like heaven to your man. Unless he has a housekeeper or lives in a hotel, this is a luxury he can't enjoy at home. You want him to enjoy being in your bed in every possible way.

Now for the fun stuff. Check out the lighting in your bedroom and bathroom and consider changing all the lightbulbs to low-wattage pink bulbs, which will make your skin look fabulous. Low-wattage bulbs also guarantee you will preserve some mystery even if the two of you end up in the tub or shower. Candles—preferably fat pillar candles arranged where they won't get knocked over—are essential, since some of the most magical and romantic evenings possible take place only by candlelight. Since you don't want to overwhelm him with scent, use primarily unscented candles, and keep the matches handy right next to them. (Don't forget to blow them out before you go to sleep!)

To finish setting the stage for sex, don't forget the practical stuff. Put condoms and lubricant, if you need it, in your bedside table drawer. If you have a table but no drawer, then find a pretty box of some kind to set on the table and store these essentials in there. You want to keep them out of sight but close at hand, so that you don't have to ruin the mood by going into the bathroom for them when they are needed

The bedroom is ready. On to the bathroom! Stand in the door and take a good look. Are there cosmetics everywhere? Little bottles of creams? Pills? Sweep them away. Put them out of sight. Throw out as much as you can. Clean the bathroom thoroughly. Examine your towels. Are you still using towels monogrammed with your ex-husband's initials? If so, relegate those babies to the rag bin. Or, if you're a widow and can't bear using them to wash the car, follow Emilie's example and simply store them away. How old are your towels? Your bathroom rugs? Do they look a bit worn, stained, or torn? If so, purchase at least one new set. Definitely invest in at least one large bath towel, somewhere between the size of a beach towel and a dining room throw rug. Men love these! And, if you can possibly afford it, purchase a couple of fluffy terry-cloth bathrobes— one for him and one for you.

If you have more than one bathroom in your home, you may want to set up the second one as a "his" bathroom, especially if your bathroom doesn't have a separate area for the toilet. We all know it's best for a man to have his own toilet, if possible!

Whether it is in a separate bathroom or a bathroom he will share with you, stock a little drawer or shelf with emergency supplies like disposable razors, shaving cream, deodorant, toothbrushes, toothpaste, and combs. Check out the sample bins at your drug store and purchase several of each item in the smallest size possible. These supplies must all be brand new! Don't ever leave the slightest hint that anyone has been there before. This, of course, requires vigilance if you do become involved with more than one gentleman at a time. You may need to put Joe's supplies in a plastic bag and hide it when Fred is expected for dinner. If a relationship fades away, throw out his bathroom supplies—along with his pillow.

Since the bathroom can be a location for romance as well as hygiene, you're not finished yet. Do you have a tub? If so, might the two of you be sharing it at some point? At the very least it should look tempting. Buy some bubble bath, bath salts, or bath oils, as well as a loofah sponge for washing his back. Purchase some wonderful soaps. And don't forget to add the most important touch, the candles. If you aren't already lighting lovely scented candles in your bathroom just for yourself, start now. It's a treat you deserve, and your man will enjoy it too.

The place is shaping up nicely; now what about you? Look in your underwear drawer. What do you see there? Is your lingerie feminine and inviting? Is it sexy? Get yourself to the lingerie department of your favorite store, or shop using a catalog or a web site, and spiff yourself up. Thongs? Push-up bras? Teddies? Buy whatever looks great, makes you feel wonderful, and gives you confidence. Replace your Chicago Bears' extra-large T-shirt you've been wearing to bed and get something slinky, like a silky nightgown (*not* pajamas). If it fits well, it will hide any flaws you might think you have.

SEXY SCENE DOS AND DON'TS

Don't use silk sheets (too slippery)

Don't use flannel sheets (too grandmotherly)

Do use 25-watt pink lightbulbs (they're flattering)

Do light candles (they smell good and create mystery)

Don't arrange fifteen little pillows on your bed (it's too fussy)

Do buy five or so pillows in a variety of sizes and types (and let him pick his own)

Do dab on a little perfume (use it sparingly, maybe only on your little toes)

Do wear a sexy new nightie (he will love it)

Don't wear your old school nightshirt (too collegiate)

Don't wear anything flannel (it's too aging)

Do play background music that you both enjoy (it sets a romantic mood)

Don't leave the television on (it's too distracting)

Do enjoy!

Ready, Set, Go!

You've prepared yourself both mentally and physically, and now you and he are ready to move on to intimacy. Hopefully, you are confident and excited, with no doubts or inhibitions. But perhaps you still have a little doubt about the naked thing? Here's a maneuver that will help. We call it "the nightie slide." Assuming that the two of you haven't become so excited and impatient that you've ripped off all of your clothes and left them on the bedroom floor (in which case you don't need this maneuver), go into the bathroom and slip out of your clothes and into your nightie. Then come bouncing into the bedroom, where hopefully he is relaxing under the covers. Now you get under the covers, too. Then you just slide your nightie over your head and drop it next to the bed, where you can retrieve it later—probably the next morning. The next morning, when unflattering daylight has flooded your room and it is finally time to reluctantly let go of each other and get up, reach down to the floor and pick up your nightie. Without getting out of bed, slide it right back over your head and then get out from under the covers! Chances are you won't feel the need to use "the nightie slide" once things get going with your man. But, sometimes it boosts our confidence just to know that this little maneuver is possible.

Since your intimacy will likely come at the end of an evening together, alcohol may be part of the picture. This is a confidence builder for many people if used in moderation. It can also destroy an evening or a mood. Many men lose their sexual ability after an evening, even a lovely one, of cocktails, wine with dinner, and after-dinner drinks. You will have to make your own decision about whether to include alcohol in your evening or not. If you do, only you can know where that fine line is between mellow or relaxing and too much. Everyone's tolerance is different. Hopefully, you know yours and your man knows his, and the two of you will have a relaxing, loving, intimate experience together.

You are ready and set. This may all seem absurd, but you are going to have fun! Keep in mind you need to:

- Suspend reality

- Live in the moment

- Focus on him

- Be creative

- Go with your gut

- Keep the *Cosmo* advice in mind

- Let yourself be a little wild—or a lot wild!

- Have an orgasm—real or fake

- Laugh a lot

- Always, always, always have fun

How Mature Women Handle the Trickiest Sex Questions

Some of our most sexually active friends and acquaintances over fifty told us about quandaries they have confronted about sex and how they have successfully addressed them. Here is a compilation of what they've discovered—often by trial and error.

Question: When is it okay to fake an orgasm?

Answer: Any time you're not having a real one and are pretty sure it just isn't going to happen this time. It will make him feel great (because he won't know), and it will make you feel pretty good, too.

Question: How much pillow talk is appropriate?

Answer: Let him be the guide, and then talk (sigh, gasp, moan, etc.) just a tiny bit more than he does. Talk in a whisper, while breathing into his ear if possible, and keep it all very sensual, positive, complimentary, and brief. "Oh, that's it." "Hmmmm, so good." "You feel wonderful." "Your touch is terrific."

Question: How do I tell him where I like it and what I like best?

Answer: The guiding principle is "show him, don't tell him." Nothing is sexier than taking his hand and moving it to the place you want him to stroke.

Question: At what point do I take time out to apply a lubricant?

Answer: You don't. You want him to think you are juiced because of him, not because of a gel in a tube. Zip off to the bathroom to apply it ahead of time—by as much as an hour or two, if necessary; lubricant lasts. Carry a small tube in your purse just in case.

Question: How do I discover his favorite places to be touched?

Answer: Listen very carefully. His breathing will tell you. It is also very sexy amidst the stroking and petting to whisper, "Show me where to touch you next."

Question: If I actually enjoy the missionary position, which I do, why should I deviate from it?

Answer: Variety really is the spice of a sex life. At least swing over on top of him every so often. If you initiate that much, he'll likely guide you into other positions from there. New locations are also a good idea: try in the shower, under the grand piano, or at the bathroom sink.

Question: What if he wants anal sex?

Answer:: Try it, if it is comfortable for you.

Question: How do I get comfortable with oral sex? It's just not my thing.

Answer: He may really enjoy this, but you know your limits, and you can always develop really good hands.

Question: What do I say if he just isn't able to get firm?

Answer: Just emphasize that you love his touch, love touching him, and are very turned on. He'll be delighted to know that he actually has given you some pleasure. Next time he might either take a pill for erectile dysfunction or drink less.

Aftermath

He's gone home now, and you are reviewing what happened. Maybe it was a peak experience: You are still glowing and maybe even doing a little dance in your kitchen. Great! It wasn't a peak experience? You wonder if you should have? You aren't sure whether he will call again or whether this will only be a temporary thing? You forgot about the condom? You feel guilty because back in your high school days "nice girls didn't"— especially not on the first date? You let him seduce you when you didn't really intend to? Nix the negative. No guilt!

Ask yourself the following:

- ❧ Did I have fun? Even for part of the time?

- ❧ Did I laugh? Even once?

- ❧ Did I live in the moment? Even for one moment?

🦋 Did I get my heart rate up? Heart health is important!

🦋 Did I learn anything? Position? Touch? Condom etiquette?

🦋 Did I survive this experience? (Obviously, you did.)

🦋 Do I feel alive! Yes!

Did you answer "yes" to any of the above questions? You did? So, if you weren't dancing around your kitchen in the afterglow of a fabulous night (as we hope you were), put on your favorite upbeat CD and start dancing now. Maybe you have just been with Mr. Forever After. Maybe you are going to have a really fun fling with Mr. For Awhile. Or maybe it was just a one-time frolic with Mr. See You Later. Maybe you don't know quite yet just which of these three guys you were with last night. But you had fun. You took care of your health. And you now know you are still a sexual being. Even if everything didn't go perfectly, you are on your way. Whether you have just started an intimate relationship with a permanent partner or you have experienced intimacy with someone more temporary, the important thing is to continue to move forward. Forever after or not, keep having fun!

Except to learn lessons that you can carry into the future, never, ever look back. Yesterday is history. It's over. You are moving on to the future!

Figuring in the Family

So you've started a full dating life, one that includes sex. Maybe your adult children are delighted for you. Or maybe not. Emilie's adult children were not happy when she started to date, even though it was almost three years after her husband's death. Their preference would have been for her to join a convent, ideally a cloistered order. A year later, when Emilie met the man who is now her significant other, her children welcomed him with blank stares and correct, but hardly friendly, behavior. It was an uphill climb that took about three years, but they did eventually warm up to her new partner.

One of the most difficult things for Emilie's children to accept—and possibly will be for yours too—was a man stepping into what they saw as their father's place, the bedroom. Fortunately, Emilie had been accepting in the past about their overnight guests. Since she had never raised a fuss, neither could they. Still, it is a difficult transition even for adult children, and it can only be worked out over time with sensitivity and understanding.

Other grown children, however, are accepting from the beginning. Audrey, widowed seventeen years ago when she was fifty-three, is a journalist who has had a number of serious flings since. She reports, "My three children and I all adored their father. But they are very close to me and somehow have always seen me as energetic and alive, so it has been easy for them to accept that I would have new men in my life. Of course, there are some they have been less happy about than others."

If you have teenagers living at home, heaven help you! Typically, teenagers are very embarrassed by their parents' divorce and especially by their mother dating, let alone doing anything else. However, there is most assuredly a different standard for fathers than for mothers. Even though her ex-husband remarried immediately after the divorce, Katherine realized she needed to keep any romantic involvement of her own out of her home, even after her teenage children went away to college. This is a strategy employed by many women, although it is not always possible. That one-in-a-million soul mate may show up, and the two of you may want to marry or live together. In this case, you will definitely want your children to accept and welcome your new partner. It isn't an easy situation, and each family has to work it out for themselves. Counseling for all of you may be the best solution.

If your new partner is a kind, considerate, thinking person who respects the boundaries of others, he will understand your children's reluctance to accept him and not feel threatened by it. If you are happy and thriving with your new partner and he is good for you, your children will see that and will eventually come around. It may take time and patience—and, in the case of teenagers, every ounce of love and perseverance you can muster as a parent—but it will happen.

You should also expect your adult children to worry about you spending your money—which they are hoping will someday become their money—on a man. This is especially true if you are a widow and they view your financial resources as "Dad's money." In this case, it is important to discuss financial arrangements with them. Also, as we'll discuss in Step 7, you'll want to consult your legal advisor about a prenuptial or cohabitation agreement. Once your children have been assured that you are not supporting this new arrival in their lives and that he is paying his fair share, this impediment to their acceptance of him will be removed.

Your children are the most important people in the world to you, and their concerns should be addressed. Listen to them and try to resolve their issues if they are making rational points, but don't let them deter you. They either already have their own lives or will have them soon. You have a right to your life, too.

The only questions you need to ask yourself are:

- Am I happy with this man?

- Do he and I laugh a lot together?

- Do we have mutual respect and consideration for each other?

- Is he kind and respectful to me and my children?

❧ Do we have a mutually satisfying sex life?

❧ Am I living a joyful life?

If you can answer yes to all these questions, you and your relationship are thriving. If a few answers are negative, however, keep on persevering. You are engaged in life and in a relationship that either will improve or will end. The important thing is that you are not sitting at home with the cat knitting a thirty-foot-long scarf! You are living life with all its ups and downs, its traumas and triumphs. You are functioning, feeling, and mostly having fun. If one relationship doesn't work, take a day to cry and mope, then get up and start all over again. Keep going no matter what.

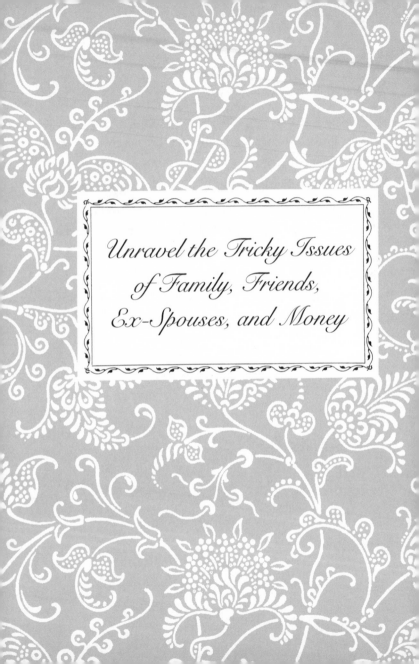

Unravel the Tricky Issues
of Family, Friends,
Ex-Spouses, and Money

7

INTO HIS ARMS OR INTO HIS LIFE

So you've met someone who piques your interest. You like him. You want to see him more often. And you want to get to know him more intimately. But is it the real thing? Is he a fling, or is he a forever after?

The Real Thing?

Let's define *real*. It means "actually being in existence, not artificial, genuine." So, ask yourself: Is there an actual relationship here? Is it genuine, or is it a fantasy? After you answer yes or no, write down your reasons. Now, let's consider the term *genuine*. Its meaning is reflected in words like "sincere" and, most importantly, "honest." Since we are applying this definition to men, rather than to diamonds, it is a bit more difficult to determine genuineness. Is he consistent? Does he call when he says he will? Or does he play the game of "Now you see me, now you don't"? Does he make plans to see you at least once a week, or does he mysteriously disappear on occasion?

Draw two columns on a sheet of paper with "sincere/honest" at the top of one and "insincere/dishonest" at the top of the other. Think about his statements and his actions within the context of your relationship and put each under one of the two columns. Did he invite you to join him in Jamaica and then mysteriously cancel? Put that under the "insincere/dishonest" column. Did he glowingly describe a business deal that skirted the edge of the law or your idea of integrity? That's another for the "insincere/dishonest" column. Did he tell you about playing golf with someone who won money by cheating and say he would never play with that person again? Put that under the "sincere/honest" column. You've got the idea. If the "sincere/honest" column is longer, you might be looking at the real deal.

Once you've completed your two columns, read what you've written. If you have been honest with yourself, you should now have at least some idea whether the relationship is "real" or not. And the answer is most likely what your gut was telling you anyway.

Carolyn's Search

A bright, successful executive and long-time divorcée with considerable dating experience, Carolyn hasn't been able to find that one kind, considerate partner because she falls over and over again for men who do not fit any definition of "real"—in fact, they're mostly con men! They wine her and dine her, causing her to laugh and exciting her on every date. Unfortunately, that excitement generally depends on the tall tales they tell about themselves. Because Carolyn badly wants each to be the real thing, she ignores signs of dishonesty and insincerity. So, although she gets high marks for being out there and having fun, the inevitable disappointments when the "real" things turn out to be the wrong things are very hard on her psyche. She bounces back each time, and we love her for that, but then along comes Mr. Not-So-Honest-But-Very-Exciting once again, and Carolyn happily takes up with him while turning her intuition off. Maybe some day Mr. Exciting will also be Mr. Real Honest. Her friends hope so.

We are all vulnerable to bad boys. After all, they are fun! It's fine to hang out with a bad boy once in a while, as long as you know what they are and why you are there. Have a good time and enjoy the excitement, but never delude yourself that this relationship is "real."

Ten Tips for Finding the Real Deal

If you are unsure about whether you've found the real deal, consider the following criteria. He might be "real" if:

1. **He introduces you:**

   To his best friend—and you pass the "friend" test.

   To his children—and they are not openly hostile.

   To his parents—and his mother does not call you by his ex-wife's name. His father might call you by the ex-girlfriend's name, but he's a dear anyway!

   To his siblings and their spouses—and his sisters and sisters-in-law do not make snide comments about your clothes, hair, or weight. In fact, a couple of them seem to like you!

2. **He remembers:**

   Christmas or Hanukkah—and he gives you presents that are thoughtful instead of practical.

   New Year's—and you go out for a great evening.

   Valentine's Day—and he plans a special evening as well as gives you a card—bonus points if he gives you a gift, too.

   Your birthday—and you didn't even have to drop hints to remind him (well, not too many anyway).

3. He goes to:

Your mother's eighty-fifth birthday party in Biloxi, Mississippi, in August, and he doesn't melt or even break a sweat—and he charms your mother completely.

Your nephew's eighth-grade football game—and he cheers loudly every time your nephew is in on a play.

Your wine and food society's six-hour-long Christmas dinner—and not only does he not get drunk, he does his best to help out during the ordeal by discussing elk hunting for two hours with one table mate.

Your office's summer picnic—and he participates cheerfully in the three-legged race and the egg toss, and he doesn't even complain when an egg breaks on his new Polo shirt.

4. He agrees:

To take care of Murphy, your eighty-pound Rottweiler, while you are out of town—and he lets Murphy sleep on his bed.

To pick you up from the airport thirty miles away—and he doesn't complain about the traffic.

To go to the drugstore for medicine when you have the flu—and he brings along with the medicine some chicken soup from the deli.

To attend your daughter's thirtieth birthday party in Chicago in January when it is 20 degrees below zero, and he buys new clothes to wear to the party, *and* he does all this despite the fact that your daughter, bless her cotton-picking little heart, has not accepted him in your life and treats him like he's not even there!

5. **He brings:**

Flowers for no special reason except to make you happy—and he is unexpectedly good at arranging them.

A special bottle of Chilean wine he found while attending a tasting at a local wine shop—and he gives a lovely toast before you take your first sip.

A fish he caught, filleted, and smoked to serve as a dinner party appetizer—plus, he sets up the bar while you are frantically preparing the main course before the guests arrive.

His completely outfitted tool box to fix your loose door-knobs, your clogged sink, your stuck window, your running toilet, and your dripping faucet.

6. **He provides you:**

A foot massage—and he brings some great smelling foot cream with him from his home.

A neck massage when you've had a really stressful day.

Tickets to a tennis tournament you've been wanting to attend, although he'd rather go to a baseball game.

A sentimental card he bought "just because."

7. He teaches you:

How to shoot skeet—and is very, very patient even though you never hit anything.

How to ice fish—and he doesn't mind that you bring a chair, wine, smoked salmon, and the Sunday *New York Times* and never pay attention to the fishing line he has carefully set up for you.

How to play golf—and he never criticizes or yells at you, even when you are playing another couple for money and you miss your putt.

How to master some of the Latin dances you've never before learned—and the two of you laugh joyfully, even if you do occasionally step on his foot.

8. He tolerates:

Your late husband's sister, who thinks you should have taken up holy orders, not a new man—and he finally charms her until she is envious instead of critical.

Your very occasional inclination to have way too much fun at a party and he gets you home safely—plus, he pulls off your cowboy boots for you when you can't get them off yourself!

Your best friend, who might be a little zany but you love her—and he really enjoys her husband, so he enjoys it when the four of you do things together.

Your children, whom you love deeply but who, truthfully, can be terrors on occasion—those occasions occurring always in his presence.

9. **He doesn't say "I told you so" when:**

You insist the after-dinner coffee is decaf—but it isn't, and both of you are awake most of the night when he has an important meeting the next morning for which he must be super-sharp.

You know your almost-senile Aunt Tilly grows mold in her refrigerator, but you tell him she has never actually poisoned anyone yet—and within hours of eating one of Aunt Tilly's dinners, the two of you are horribly ill.

You proudly announce you are saving money by coloring your hair yourself instead of paying $75 to your colorist, and your hair turns orange—but he still takes you out to dinner at a dark, intimate restaurant.

You tell him with absolute confidence that his favorite team is *not* playing football on Monday night, so he agrees to go to a chick flick with you instead—but he learns afterward that not only did his team play on Monday, but they engineered a big upset.

10. He comforts you when:

You back your car through the garage door—and he gets the repair estimates for both the car and the door!

Your dress is too tight—and he brushes it off by saying he never liked that color on you anyway.

You get a bad haircut and wish you could hide—and he says he thinks the change is sexy.

Your dog dies and he brings you a special frame with a photo of your faithful friend—plus, he doesn't mind that you keep the dog's ashes under your bed.

If he does some of the above for you, *and* you do the same for him, it's real! You've achieved a mutually supportive relationship of equals who respect, honor, and take care of one another.

∼⌒

I had done a lot of dating and been married for over twenty years before my divorce, but I never knew what it was like to be truly loved until I met Jim. We are so happy and comfortable together and take good care of each other. He is the kindest man I have ever known.

—KAREN, 61, ADMINISTRATIVE ASSISTANT

So this may be it. You two are a couple, and it looks like you have a future. Congratulations: You've found a forever after. However, there are still a few things to work out.

His Family and How to Charm Them

However much you may wish otherwise sometimes, the two of you don't exist in a vacuum. He has a family, and perhaps a large one. If he is lucky, his parents are still living, and he most likely has siblings who have their own families. He might have children, either adults or teenagers. He may also have former in-laws to whom he is close. He has probably been married at least once, and his family certainly knew and probably liked the previous wife.

THE PREVIOUS WIFE

If your guy is a widower, you will have to deal with the specter of his previous wife, who has now been elevated to sainthood. That's just the way it is, and it won't change. There is no point in trying to compete with her, so don't try. If she made fabulous brownies, you perfect an apple pie. If she was a wonderful housekeeper, you become a master gardener. You don't need to feel threatened, and you can afford to be gracious. The heart is infinitely expandable, and his continuing love for her does not negate his love for you. Never must a disparaging word about this good woman cross your lips or, if at all possible, your thoughts. Instead, make it easy for her family to mention her in front of you by making comments like, "She must have been wonderful. I wish I had known her." His family members want him to find someone with whom he can share his life. Your job is to make sure they see you as that someone, so just be yourself and focus on your relationship. There will be a third person in that relationship, but she will be a friendly ghost if you allow her.

All bets are off, however, if he has an ex-wife rather than a late wife. An ex can, and she certainly might, make all sorts of trouble. Hopefully she has moved on and is not interested in you or your relationship with her ex. However, some divorced people seem to love to aggravate each other. His family know her, and they may like her very much. Some of his siblings as well as his parents might still include her in family events, especially if there are children, even adult children, involved.

Your situation will largely depend on how or why the marriage ended. If your sweetheart was the injured party, his family members will probably welcome you as long as they can see that you are "good for him." If there are children nearby, you will find yourself at social events that include the ex and possibly her present husband. Although you might want a stiff drink on these occasions very badly, do not give in to temptation. Wait until you get home. Simply be friendly and charming, no matter what. These situations are a test of your character. Do not fail the test!

Your guy and his ex might be very friendly, although this, too, can provide its own challenge. Obviously it's nice if they don't antagonize each other in social situations, but if they're too close or spend too much time together it may seem nauseating to you. Talk with your man in private. Tell him what bothers you and why. If he really is the man for you, he will want to understand and work through this annoyance. If he doesn't understand the situation, then you can simply limit the number of times you are present for these occasions. Let some time pass. The situation may resolve itself or cease to bother you once you become accustomed to it.

HIS PARENTS AND SIBLINGS

Whether your man is divorced or widowed, his parents and siblings are going to be predisposed to liking you. They want him to be happy and well cared for. They will hopefully see that you are a good person, that you love him, and that you are kind and considerate. Be yourself, and they will eventually see that his life is better for having you in it. They may love his late wife and grieve her passing. Or they may maintain a relationship with his ex-wife and her current husband. Whichever is the case, be kind and loving toward them, and they will return the same to you. If they don't, be kind and loving anyway. You have nothing to lose, and your special man will love you for it.

HIS PREVIOUS WIFE'S FAMILY

Whether your guy is widowed or divorced, his previous wife's parents, siblings, and maybe even cousins, aunts, and uncles might be very much in his life. This is especially so if he is a widower with adult children living nearby or children still living at home. His siblings, especially sisters, and particularly those who live near him, may not welcome you with open arms. It is often strange for them to see someone in the place where they were accustomed to seeing their sister.

Even one of our nicest, kindest, most understanding friends, finding herself in this situation, said, "My niece asked me to have dinner with her father, his new wife, her brother, and herself. I did, and the new wife is a nice lady. But I like my sister better."

In time, the siblings will see that you have no intention of interfering in their relationship with their nieces and nephews and that their brother-in-law was lucky to find you. All you can really do is hang on and be pleasant. In the case where a family member has died, you cannot win except by treating her relatives with the utmost courtesy and, if they let you, affection. You, of course, do not have to stand for hostile treatment from them. But if you find them unpleasant to deal with, your options are pretty limited, and the best one is simply to limit your contact with them.

In the case of family members left over from a divorce, like the ex-wife's brother whom your guy has season football tickets with and whose company he genuinely enjoys, it is easier for you to set boundaries for yourself. No one has died, and, even in the most cordial divorces, your guy and his ex don't like each other that well or they would still be married. The difficulty for you is that everything you say, do, and wear is going to be minutely observed, dissected, and reported straight back to the ex. Your hair, your makeup, and your weight (whether too much or too little of all three) will be thoroughly discussed—not by your guy's male buddy, who couldn't care less, but by his wife and the ex and her female siblings.

The same scenario may also occur with a couple that you see together socially. The wife of the couple may be a good friend of your guy's ex-wife. If this troubles you, you can limit your contact with these people while encouraging the two men to continue their buddy activities. You can be "busy" on proposed couple occasions until the social contact peters out for lack of momentum, and it will. When you are in uncomfortable situations you cannot avoid, be socially polite, be distant, and keep repeating to yourself, "I am a lady, I am a lady, I am a lady!" You will not only be a lady, you will be a winner.

Mixing and Matching His Friends and Yours

Every new couple has to sort out their friends. There will be some that stick and some that won't. Both of you have your very best long-time friends: you can't imagine life without yours, and he can't imagine life without his. He has his buddies he hunts with, plays poker with, plays golf or basketball with, or has season tickets with, and he is not going to give them up. You have your girlfriends you lunch with, talk long hours with, laugh and cry with, and play golf, tennis, or bridge with, and you are not going to give them up. At the same time, however, you both have couples that you have always known and done things with who also know your previous spouse or significant other. They may still be keeping up that relationship as well as the relationship with you and your man. This can be awkward.

After a divorce friends fall into one of three categories: the ones that stick with you, the ones that stick with your ex, and those with divided loyalties. Your friends with divided loyalties don't pose much of a problem for your new guy when he meets them because, with few exceptions, men don't talk about personal stuff that much and aren't likely to pass along any information beyond "Seems like a nice guy." But women, if they are still good friends with the ex, will talk about you no matter how much they genuinely like you and how nice they are to you. It's probably best not to share girlfriends with the ex if you can avoid it, unless you're the lucky woman who isn't made uncomfortable by this situation.

Explaining to your man why you are uncomfortable socializing with certain people isn't easy because he can't relate to the problem. It is usually best to be straightforward and simply say, "I know it seems strange to you, but it is uncomfortable for me to socialize with friends of your ex-wife, even though they are nice people and very friendly. It is just the nature of women to talk, and they are all friends of your ex, so I am sure they are discussing me with her. I'd like to see them less frequently, and I'd like for us to start making new friends as well as seeing the old." You can then let time take its course. Eventually you will discover that you are seeing more of the new friends and those that you both feel comfortable with and less of the others.

If your man is a widower, all his friends will hopefully be supportive of the new relationship and delighted that he has found someone. Expect the women in the group to compare you to his late wife. With any luck, they will not go on too much about the dearly departed, rhapsodizing about her perfect house, her perfect children, her hugely successful career, her culinary expertise, and the close, totally loving relationship she had with your man! As with relatives, though, your only option is to agree with all of the statements lauding the late wife, smile, nod, and leave their company as soon as possible. Hopefully, most of them will be delighted for their friend and, although they are grieving the loss of their dear girlfriend, will accept you in time. Some of them may even become good friends of yours.

There is one final category of friends who you will like a lot: those who never did like the ex! These friends are to be cherished. The women will tell you all about the ex's faults, and you will discover you enjoy hearing about them. Once they've revealed their feeling, you may be able to develop friendships with these people, who hopefully will like you much better.

In conclusion, you will have friends that mix and friends that don't mix. Nurture the first group and ease out the second. Some examples of his friends that don't mix are:

- ❧ **Charlie, "The Chuckster":** His old college frat brother who is loud, drinks too much, and makes sexist remarks. Cut him out of your life quickly. Suggest they meet for lunch during the week.

- ❧ **Bland Bob:** His office colleague, single, nice, and very dull. Here is a chance to fix up your very nice, slightly dull, and very talkative girlfriend. At least if they get together, you won't need to.

- ❧ **Ever-present Evan:** His good buddy whose wife is the best friend of his ex. Ease away from him gradually; everyone will be happier for it. He and his buddy can do things without you.

- ❧ **The Weekend Travel Club:** His friends who mean well but will not stop talking about the "old" days, before your arrival on the scene, and all the fun they had together. Let him know the reminiscing strikes you as rude and boring. And if he won't do anything about it, let the whole group know—pleasantly, if you want to continue seeing them, firmly, if you don't.

His friends that do mix include:

- His friends who want him to be happy and welcome you with warmth and friendliness. Go slow and let them come to you, accepting their overtures in the manner given.

- His friends who never liked the ex anyway. Nurture the friendship by making plans for an evening out.

- His friends whom you genuinely like and want to get to know. Invite them to dinner now!

- His friends whom you can easily integrate with your friends because they have interests in common. Throw a party so that some of his friends and some of yours can meet and mingle.

Your Friends—to Mix or Not

Admit it. Your friends aren't all perfect either. All of the above criteria for determining whether they can be integrated into your new relationship apply to them, too. The only difference is that you are less likely to have to worry about them gossiping.

Apply the same criteria to your friends that you apply to his and listen to what he has to say about them. Are there some girlfriends he doesn't like? Does he describe anyone as "flaky" or "snobby" or "wacky"? If so, try to find out what he really means. Do they make him feel bored? Uncomfortable? Unwelcome?

We girlfriends can be very protective of each other, and, if we have any doubts about the new man in our friend's life, we may not be as warm and welcoming as we will be once he proves to be kind, loving, and good for our friend. We can all relate to Alice, who was not enthusiastic about Marsha's new man. Although she was outwardly cordial to him, she thought Marsha could do better and told her so. He picked up on Alice's attitude, however, and, when the relationship proved to be a permanent one for Marsha, Alice had to work hard to overcome the negative impression she had created.

You may have a few really close girlfriends whom you can't live without but he can. Chances are you already see each other most of the time without your partners, so keep on doing this, but also try to get him to agree to attend some events with your girlfriends and their husbands, boyfriends, or significant others. If he likes your girlfriends' partners, he may be more willing to go along with social plans that include some of the women he could do without.

Under *no* circumstances should you cut yourself off from your dear women friends just because he wants your full attention or doesn't approve of them. Unless they are leading you astray into prostitution, shoplifting, or any other criminal enterprise, hang onto them for dear life. You've been enjoying each other's company for years now. And, even though you have this fascinating new man in your life and, therefore, less time for your girlfriends than before, you still need them to be part of your life. Women friends add to our lives significantly by providing emotional and psychological nurturing in a way even our much-loved husbands and significant others just can't.

Rebecca's Reality

Our dear friend Rebecca, a retired nurse and independent-minded widow, fell hard and fast as soon as mutual friends introduced her to Morrie, an automobile salesman and handsome widower of many years. Fortunately, he felt the same about her, and they were quickly totally involved with each other and the excitement of their romance. They each wanted to make a deep commitment to the other, and they did. Afterward, their previous friends saw them only infrequently. Rebecca's friends were sad that a valued relationship seemed to be slipping away. After a few years, when the newness and excitement, but not the commitment and love, had settled a little, Rebecca and Morrie both realized that their respective same-sex friends had roles to play in their lives too. Rebecca came down with a serious case of pneumonia, causing her girlfriends to rally to her side with nourishing chicken soup for her and meals for Morrie, as well as their love and support while she recovered. Now Rebecca makes more time for her girlfriends, whom she realizes she needs to be part of her life. She tells everyone that the nurturing, support, and laughter that women bring to each other are essential to us all.

His Prized Possessions and How to Deal with Them

You and he are in each other's arms so much you are effectively living together. Maybe you have just drifted into this state, or perhaps it was a conscious decision. Perhaps you have decided to marry, or perhaps not. You'll discover that combining households, like combining friends, can be tricky. You both have lots of stuff, and some of it is near and dear to your heart. You have your grandmother's bedroom set, complete with twin beds and an antique vanity table. He has his collection of stuffed elk, deer, antelope, and moose heads! No way is he having fussy antiques in his bedroom—especially not if it means twin beds! And, no way are you going to live with dead animals staring at you! What to do?

Here are some possibilities:

- Manage to "lose" a few things while moving. Emilie was good at this during her marriage. Every time she and her husband moved, a few pieces of furniture or memorabilia got "lost," including a five-foot-high tiki he bought in Hawaii and an ugly faux Spanish chest from his first marriage.

- Place his offending items somewhere you won't see them too often. How about putting his favorite hunting trophies in his basement workroom? The den where he and his buddies watch football but you hardly ever go? Could his twelve framed prints of ships be scattered about various guest bathrooms and the laundry room? After all, these are all rooms having to do with water.

- Convince him to rent out his place with most of his furniture in it. If the two of you do move into your home, you will be more in control of what stays, what goes, and what he brings. Of course, you will have to make some compromises, because he needs to feel at home, so perhaps one hunting trophy or his aunt's ugly antique lamp with the fringed shade will have to find a spot in your home somewhere.

- Temporarily store his things, and maybe some of yours, in a self-storage locker. Put items you cannot find a place for into it as a "temporary" situation. He will probably forget about some or all of them in a while, and they can just live in storage forever.

- If possible, establish "his" and "hers" rooms. Your grandmother's bedroom set can occupy a guest room, and you can get a nice king- or queen-sized bed with a pillow-top mattress for the master bedroom. His casual living room furniture, complete with his ten paintings of famous

Indian chiefs and collection of beer steins, could be perfect for the family room.

🦋 Keep working on it, and you will eventually find a solution that's comfortable for both of you. You both want to keep some of your dearest possessions around you and, because you love each other, will learn to love each other's stuff. One couple we know is fortunate enough to be able to have a winter and a summer place in two different states. Hers is the winter place; his is the summer. They are each in charge of furnishing their own place, and they happily live in the other's home half the year. This elegant solution isn't available to everyone, however. You will find your own creative way to combine your homes and stuff. Give it time. Be patient. It will fall into place. You may even become fond of the stuffed moose head!

Tricky Financial Issues

Financial issues start raising their ugly head when you first do something big together, like take a vacation or make a major joint purchase. These issues become even more important when you make the big decision to live together. Since you aren't two young kids starting out with nothing, those issues, though decidedly unromantic, need to be discussed and decided upon in advance. And even if who pays for what isn't important to you, it absolutely will be to your children. Hopefully, you are happily ensconced in a partnership between two equals. Each of you is going to carry your share of the load financially, as well as emotionally. Although you and your Mr. Perfect should work out a financial system that's comfortable for you and your circumstances, here are a few tips.

VISIT YOUR LAWYER

Laws about marriage and cohabitation vary by state, so it's essential you have a chat with your attorney, even if you feel you have few assets to protect. If you are getting married, you need a prenuptial agreement that spells out who gets what in the event you divorce or one of you precedes the other in death. If your intended balks at such an agreement, consider it a huge red flag. Even if you are simply living together, a cohabitation agreement is a good idea. This is especially wise in states that are common-law marriage states. Again, your attorney can tell you about the laws of your state that apply to your situation and advise you concerning the type of agreement you and your partner need to have.

THE HOUSE

The two of you are now living in one house—yours, his, or perhaps one you've rented or purchased together. How you handle expenses related to the house may depend upon whether the house belongs to one of you or to both of you. If it is your house and he has no financial interest in it, it is not unreasonable for you to pay the mortgage and real estate taxes, but he still needs to contribute in some way. If he is handy, he may do the repairs and necessary upkeep as well as the yard work. Or, the two of you might work out a reasonable contribution he makes to the mortgage. After all, he would have to pay rent or a mortgage somewhere if he weren't living in your house. If you have moved into his house, perhaps your role as the primary "keeper upper" of the home will suffice as your contribution, or you might contribute to his mortgage payments. If the two of you purchased or rented a home together, you may have decided to split everything equally, taking turns paying the rent or mortgage. Before you purchase, get advice from an attorney concerning the appropriate way to hold title to the property together and the consequences of various ownership arrangements.

HOUSEHOLD EXPENSES

Household expenses, such as groceries and utilities, should be shared by both of you. The simplest way is to establish a household kitty to which you both contribute an equal amount that is used to buy groceries and pay the utility bills as well as anything else you both want it to cover. This works well only if you are both in roughly equal financial circumstances. If one of you is accustomed to a significantly more expensive lifestyle than the other and wants to maintain that lifestyle, then the household kitty contribution might need to be adjusted according to each person's financial ability.

Emilie was accustomed to grocery shopping at the local independent market. Although the prices could be a bit higher than at the big supermarket, it was more conveniently located, was managed by pleasant people, had no checkout lines, and sold organic beef and chicken. Emilie's significant other shopped the sales at the large chain supermarket. They compromised by determining what groceries "ought" to cost and splitting that. Emilie took his contribution but continued to shop at the local market and bought what she wanted by increasing her own contribution.

There are all kinds of ways to tweak the system, as long as you both contribute and you both are comfortable with the system you come up with. The key is that each of you needs to be satisfied with the contribution the other is making. He is not a "sugar daddy," and you are not a "sugar mama."

VACATIONS

Whether you are married, living together, or just dating exclusively, you will probably decide to take a vacation together. In the excitement of planning a fun getaway, don't forget to work out who pays for what. Usually this is determined in part by who invited whom. If he invited you to join him at a fabulous resort where he is attending a conference, chances are he has made all the arrangements and you are his guest at the resort. He may also arrange for and pay for your plane ticket. Whether he does or whether this is important to you is something only you can decide. You may want to provide your own transportation simply in order to maintain some independence. Since he has invited you, you can assume he intends to treat you to all food and entertainment expenses. But, of course, it is always elegant to treat him to dinner one night to show your appreciation. By the same token, if you invite him to your mother's eighty-fifth birthday party in Miami, you should be prepared to foot the bill. After all, he is doing you a huge favor.

If you are planning a trip together just for fun and decide to split vacation expenses equally, you should have an equal say in where you stay, where you eat, and what you do. When Emilie and her significant other travel, she prefers four-star hotels, while he is fine with any motel that is clean. On the other hand, they both like four-star restaurants. On vacation, then, she pays for the accommodations, and he pays for the meals. Creative thinking will lead you to a solution that works for you. And if the financial arrangements are worked out in advance, you can relax, enjoy yourselves, and concentrate on having fun.

Necessary Closeness and (Equally) Necessary Distance

Congratulations: You are a couple. You are close. You communicate fabulously and work out decisions that are mutually agreeable to you both. You have a great, supportive, loving relationship.

But in order for your relationship to thrive for the many years ahead, you will also need some distance in your relationship. You are two individuals as well as a couple, and you are not superglued to each other. You can do things without each other, and it is important that you do. You can still belong to your bridge group and your book group. He can still belong to his poker group and his golfing group. He can go fishing with the boys, and you can go to a beach house with the girls. He can visit his mother without you (in fact, his mother would probably love some time alone with him). You can each visit your children and grandchildren without the other one. And you should. As much as your children and grandchildren may like your new partner, they still need you to themselves on occasion. If holiday plans conflict, it's okay to split up. You can go help out your daughter who has just had a baby and is desperately in need of someone to make the Thanksgiving dinner. He can have a Thanksgiving visit with his son and daughter-in-law who have just bought a new house they are dying for him to see. You do not have to lead your lives in lockstep. His grandson's hockey games do not hold the same fascination for you they do for him. Your granddaughter's ballet recital is not his first choice for Sunday afternoon entertainment. You do not have a master/slave relationship, and no one should set the agenda for the other.

Doing things separately does not suggest a lack of love, but doing things only together may suggest a lack of common sense. By acknowledging that something important to you might bore him to death and by giving him a graceful way out, you demonstrate your love and respect for him. Doing this will only enhance the closeness you have during the rest of the time you are together. If you truly have a relationship that is the real thing, respecting each other's boundaries allows you to be secure in the knowledge that both of you will always wing your way back to each other.

You've determined you and your special man have the real thing. He's good to you, and you're good to him. You've worked out difficulties with your family, friends, and financial issues. Grab that brass ring and don't look back. Life is joyful; live every minute!

*Gain Momentum
with Attitude
and a Plan*

8

COMMIT TO IT

*M*OMENTUM MATTERS! Building relationships with men is like pitching snowballs downhill; they gather more volume and speed as they tumble. Once you get rolling, more and more good things—good men, to be exact—come your way. This is because attracting and relating to a particular guy are a process, not an event. You start the process, stick with it, and momentum builds.

We realize you won't get up tomorrow morning and begin to put every idea in this book into action at once. You probably have already figured out that achieving relationship success requires you not only to work through the steps we outline, but also to adapt our suggestions, feel your way along, use your intuition, and regroup from time to time. But to begin the process tomorrow, you need to make a commitment today.

Reflection on what you have read so far is good, but action is better. To support that action, we suggest you develop an attitude and make a plan. Unless you do both, you'll be left back where you were when you opened this book: hoping for fulfilling relationships with men but floundering in your attempts to make that happen. Think of anything you might want for yourself: a new career, a college or graduate degree, a new house, a small business on the side, a major travel adventure, or one or more new men in your life. To tackle any of these goals in a serious way, you first need to develop the can-do, will-do attitude that allows you to get started and, importantly, to persist no matter what. Next, you need to develop the plan that will guide your efforts.

There's Attitude in Those Steps

We've suggested that you take many actions in this book, but behind every successful action also is your attitude: a way of viewing your situation and your needs that gives you the mental fortitude to move forward. From a number of themes that recur throughout this book, we have distilled eight key "attitude boosters"—perspectives that will support you in your successful action at every step along the way.

1. **Start Your Engines!** The phrase is almost overused, but it's true: "Fifty is the new thirty." We are not our mothers or grandmothers, nor are we slowly becoming them. At fifty-

plus, most of us are blessed with better health, better education, better energy, and better financial resources than our mothers and grandmothers ever dreamed of. All of that, plus we have a better understanding of what we want. And what we want isn't limited to visits from the grandchildren and the opportunity to knit another crib blanket.

Fifty-plus is our time to build a future, try new things, go places, learn, and grow. Don't waste the opportunity that our grandmothers never had: get going now and try everything that comes your way; then go out and find the things that didn't come your way. Katherine was in her mid-fifties when a dozen of her freshman college students asked her to join them in a class bonding experience: rock climbing. After she had pushed and pulled her way to the thirty-five-foot mark on a sixty-five-foot climbing wall, she had not only climbed higher than any of her eighteen-year-old students, but she had also discovered a new sport she wanted to continue to pursue.

A get-going attitude requires a sense of adventure. There will be setbacks. There will be things you try that don't work out (and nowhere is this more possible than in relationships with men). The women we talked to about their successes with men have this in common: they treat every disappointment as an interesting surprise and every surprise as an adventure. When the guy Ginny saw regularly for about five months turned out to be a frog with no prince deep down inside, she moved on; but she still continues to pursue the passion for opera that he introduced into her life. Elise is delighted to have two close new female friends she met through Paul. "Paul was a long-distance romance who turned out to be wrong for me, which was painful for a while, but these two fascinating ladies always will be in my network of close friends and fun people. One introduced me to power walking, the other to sushi."

The idea here is to keep getting up and growing no matter what. A sense of adventure helps you do that, because it heightens your optimism, your energy, and your desire to learn. Even better, it helps you laugh a lot.

2. **We're All from Pluto.** They call men and women opposite sexes for good reason, but in one very important way, we're similar: He's imperfect, and you're imperfect. That goes for both what is on the outside and what is on the inside.

The outside needs little elaboration here, because if, at this age, you think you can find someone reminiscent of Michelangelo's David, we can only hope you have bad eyesight. Instead, the guys you're considering probably are sprouting hair in weird places. So what? The same happens to you, which is why they invented tweezers. Men make more trips to the bathroom than you thought could possibly be necessary; so do you. And their skin tone is nowhere near the ideal of a baby's bottom; ditto for you. You get the drift: This is all small stuff. Don't sweat it. Care about your appearance and be in the best physical shape possible for the sake of your health and energy. Expect the same from him. But don't expect perfection from either of you.

With respect to the inside, we all know that men are very different from women. Typically, their emails are short, their conversations are to the point, and their classic line, "I'll call you," means sometime before they die. Half the men who become interested in you are afraid that you just want to get married. The other half are concerned that you seem too independent. And they could present evidence of similar confusing responses from us!

The bottom line is this: Men need us in their lives to spice things up, add humor, and introduce romance. We need them in our lives to settle things down, add humor, and introduce romance. Whether they are our friends, our significant others, or our spouses, men can make us feel very good about ourselves, and we can do the same for them. They love compliments; we love compliments. They need support for their ideas and sympathy. Ditto for us.

The best relationships are built on recognizing similarities and enjoying differences. Lighten up before you give up.

*When someone doesn't seem to be caring for you
in exactly the way you want him to, he still may
be caring for you with all he has.*

—JUNE, 63, RETIRED TEACHER

3. **Get What You Came For.** It is finally all about *you*. You get
to determine what you want in a relationship. It may be
companionship, crazy laughter, adventure travel, a shared
home, or a traditional marriage. It may also be a quick flirtation at an airport bar, an exchange of steamy emails, or a
one-night stand. At your age, you get to decide.

Once you identify what you want in a relationship, you
are likely to know it when you see it and know it when you
don't see it. You become less vulnerable to friends who
eagerly share their advice about what you should do, how
you should do it, and even whom you should do. They
may wonder why you put up with Jim, the silent and staid
widower who never wants to take you out to dinner. They
may be puzzled at your disinterest in George, the silver-
maned retired banker who loves wine tastings and sailing.
They may never understand why you enjoy overweight and
loud Chuck for your mixed-doubles tennis partner. But
they are not you. You have your own relationship chemistry and relationship intent. Sure, you should always be
open to surprises. Maybe you will like life in a mountain

cabin or on a farm better than you thought. Maybe you don't need as much time socializing with friends or as many evenings alone as you once surmised. Maybe you can adjust to being the roommate he wants rather than the romantic mate you visualized. But if a situation doesn't match up with your goals, examine it immediately with a critical eye. Most likely, if it doesn't meet your expectations now, it will not do so in the future.

Too many women compromise too quickly because they only know they want a man. They haven't spent enough time figuring out what qualities are most important to them, so when they meet a willing man they just slip under his arm and disappear into his life. Soon, however, his life is looking a little uneventful and dull. In fact, it isn't looking like anything they would have planned for themselves. Don't waste your time this way. A better opportunity is on the way.

4. **When the Going Gets Tough, the Tough Get Going to Their Girlfriends.** And their sisters, cousins, mothers, and daughters. There is no substitute for a great girlfriend— one who has seen us in all our incarnations, from savvy and capable to scared and lost. We have always needed a bunch of female buddies who know us well and support us in various ways. As single women after midlife, we need them more than ever. Who else will help you shovel through the snow in your backyard to dig a grave when

your cat dies? Who else comes to divorce court with you and gives your ex-husband the evil eye on the way out? Who else dons rubber gloves up to her elbows to spend an entire day cleaning your refrigerator and stove when you move to a new house? Who else drives an hour to your house at midnight to deliver her copy of *When Bad Things Happen to Good People* after one of your parents is diagnosed with a terminal condition?

Treasure these wonderful ladies. They cheer and applaud in the good times; they pass the hankie in the bad times. In between they are sources of laughter, energy, support, and ideas. They may or may not become instrumental in leading us to the men we enjoy, but they help give us our us-ness. With them, we share experiences, ideas, advice, and empathy; and, by doing so, we get to know ourselves better. Do they nag and give unsolicited advice too much? You bet. Do they get angry at us and put us on their "do not call" lists from time to time? Sure. But the caring underneath these friendships is unconditional and forever.

Reciprocation is absolutely essential, of course. Our best friends are there for us, and so we need to be there for them. You attend to existing friends, and you make new friends. Some move away, but they never move out of your mind and heart. Great friendship with women promotes a sense of connection that nurtures your confidence, your optimism, your vitality, and your continuing personal development—characteristics you need if you want to attract the men who are right for you.

5. **Walk Firmly but Carry a Soft Handkerchief.** You can be vulnerable sometimes and still survive. You do not have to be a tough, hard, steely-eyed woman with all of your defenses mortared into a brick wall for protection. Yes, exposing your vulnerability means you may get hurt. But you've already survived hurts and disappointments in life, and you are still standing!

At some point you will need to take a risk in a relationship. That risk may be required at the very beginning of a relationship, like it was for Karen, who happened to run into her high school boyfriend in a restaurant some forty years after graduation. Both of them were divorced, so Karen took a chance, called him up, and invited him over for a home-cooked meal. The flame was rekindled, the romance flourished, and the relationship grew into the greatest love either of them had ever known.

You may need to risk showing your feelings after the relationship has been humming along for a while in order to find out where he stands or to move from the movie-and-dinner stage to the home-by-the fire stage. Emilie took that risk, uniquely whispering "I love you" into her now significant other's ear while watching the bull riding event at a rodeo in Cheyenne, Wyoming. Seemingly struck by a sudden attack of deafness, no response was immediately forthcoming from the object of her affection. When it did come, it was, "What did you say?" Emilie responded, "Tell you later." And she did, much later, but with far greater success.

Although it might scare you to show your vulnerability, once in awhile you will have to be brave and take the plunge anyway or your guy will not know you care. If you keep the wall up, the relationship cannot progress because you will remain two strangers who have just been introduced and are making polite conversation. He needs to know you, and you need to know him, or you cannot connect. In order for that to happen, you must reveal yourselves to each other. Hopefully, you will both like what you see. If not, you will find out sooner rather than later and save yourself from becoming bogged down in a situation that isn't going anywhere anyway. So, go ahead, let yourself be open and vulnerable on occasion. It's a winning situation.

6. **Hearts Know.** Yes, you need to get organized, think about your goals, and form a plan for finding a partner and establishing a relationship, but you need to listen to your heart, too. That mysterious thing called instinct is often right on target. Subtle cues that we take into account without even thinking about it play a part in our instinctive attraction to an individual. When two hearts connect,

they both know it. Maybe it's brain waves, maybe it's pheromones, maybe it's kismet.

Sometimes you need to listen to your heart, but not to the point of turning off your brain. What the heart knows the mind ought to support too. Your brain keeps your heart from leading you into unproductive situations and from making regrettable decisions. The heart keeps the brain from constantly overanalyzing and finding fault. You've got them both, so use them both.

Occasionally, you want your heart to rule. You want romance and joie de vivre, springtime and music, sunshine and roses, even though your brain is telling you it is all too good to be true. Go ahead. Live in the moment. Suspend reality for a day or evening, but don't do it permanently. When you come back to earth, your brain will have a conversation with your heart, and you will determine whether it's too good to be true. If it's the real thing, the thinking part of you will know it as well as your heart. It will be love.

7. **Stick to Your Guns.** Repeat to yourself, "I am worth it!" You are a worthy person. You deserve kind, loving, respectful treatment from everyone in your life, and especially the men you meet, date, and fall in love with. You are allowed to set boundaries that determine what you will and will not do in various aspects of your life. You do not need to accept less than respectful treatment from anyone, including your

special man, his family, your family, his friends, or anyone else you come into contact with.

Often women are socialized to meet everyone else's needs before their own. Somewhere in between the demands of our jobs and the demands of our families, we got lost. We have learned not to recognize or think about our own needs and desires because we have no time to do anything about them anyway. Our desire has been to please everyone—our boss, our co-workers, our families.

Ask yourself:

"Who am I?"

"What do I really want?"

"What makes me happy?"

"What kind of treatment do I expect from others?"

You do not have to tolerate anyone who is dishonest or disrespectful or does not treat you like the worthwhile person you are. If you are kind, loving, considerate, and respectful toward him, you deserve the same treatment in return. You want a loving relationship between equal partners. You can set boundaries that he respects and respect his own boundaries in return. You are not his slave who cooks, cleans, and does the laundry while he sits around, and he is not your sugar daddy. You share a life together, each contributing equally.

It is okay to meet your own needs before someone else's as long as you stop short of absolute selfishness.

Some situations call for compromise, some for assertiveness. If he is great about attending the ballet with you, you will want to be gracious about going to the basketball game with him. If he goes duck hunting for a week with his buddies every fall, then he should not object to you going to a spa with your girlfriends that same week. He may not want to go with you every time you visit your daughter and her four kids, two of whom are still in diapers. And you may not want to accompany him every time he visits his son and his three loud, rather undisciplined teenage boys. This is perfectly fine. It's okay to be independent within a relationship.

And if the relationship does not work out, don't stay in it because you are afraid to move on. If your needs are not being met, or your expectations are not being fulfilled, get up, get out, get going! Don't settle for anything less than what makes you happy.

8. **Live, Love, and, Above All, Laugh. Laugh!** It's free. It's not fattening. It can't be taxed. And you absolutely can't do it enough. People who laugh a lot have better immune systems, recover from diseases more quickly, live longer, and are a whole lot happier. Finding something to laugh about at least once in each day is essential to a healthy mind and body.

Life is absurd. You know that. And what could be more absurd than dating after age fifty? You never expected to be in this somewhat awkward position. You are a grown woman, maybe even a grandmother, and here you are reliving your teenage dating years. Absurd? You bet! Something to laugh about? Oh, yes!

Love! We have plenty of opportunities to give and receive it. We have family—parents, children, grandchildren, siblings, nieces and nephews, aunts and uncles, cousins, and on and on—and we have our dear friends. We even have our pets—dogs, cats, birds, horses—whom we love and who we believe love us. For some of us, the love we give to and receive from God also sustains us. And, if we want it and we persist in looking for it, we can have that special partner with whom to share a special loving relationship. Our capacity to give and receive love is limitless. And love is so easy to find if we are open to looking for it. Never pass up an opportunity to give love. And, if you have to make a choice, this is one gift that is a whole lot better when you give it than when you receive it, although that is pretty wonderful too.

Live! The world is a big place full of limitless possibilities, so grab all that it has to offer. There are fun times to be had, new people to meet, new skills to learn, and new places and things to see. Embrace it all and refuse to accept boundaries, limits, or preconceived notions about who you are or ought to be. Be brave. Overcome your fears. You are going to soar.

Plan It, Write It, Do It

The best way to commit yourself to a course of action is in writing. That's why the buff little twenty-two-year-old trainer at your fitness center insists on creating a written checklist of the exercises she has suggested for your workout routine. Although she may surmise that your failing memory prevents you from recalling more than three exercises, she also knows you can always use an extra push to stick with the program. When you pull out the list later, she knows you'll either feel good or feel guilty about your persistence and progress. A plan in writing is a sort of contract with yourself—a commitment to do what you want to do anyway.

We suggest you write up a plan that matches you and your preferences by following the steps that guide you through this book. Here is an outline; you fill in the blanks.

STEP 1

I will take the following new actions in order to improve me on the outside. (List at least two goals, with a start date for each.)

_____

_____

_____

I will take the following new actions in order to improve me on the inside. (List at least two goals, with a start date for each.)

_____

_____

I will say "goodbye" to this (for example, a place, a habit, or a routine) from my old life. (Give yourself a deadline.)

_____

_____

STEP 2

I will increase my interactions with the following friends and family members in ways that encourage them to serve as important resources for meeting my goals. (List at least six names, and give yourself a one-year deadline.)

_____   _____

_____   _____

_____   _____

I will do these small things just for me. (List three things, and give yourself a six-month deadline.)

_____

_____

_____

I will make the following major change(s) in my personal
and/or professional life. (List one or more things, and include
a deadline for the change.)

_____

_____

STEP 3

This is the type of relationship I want with a man at this point
in my life. (Think of a continuum, with temporary companionship at one end and lifelong commitment at the other.)

_____

_____

The man who is part of that relationship will have the
following characteristics. (List at least twelve characteristics
that are very important to you.)

_____   _____

_____   _____

_____   _____

_____   _____

_____   _____

_____   _____

The following are the things we will do together. (List everything you want to do with a companion, from gardening to travel, from sports to reading.)

_____   _____

_____   _____

_____   _____

_____   _____

_____   _____

_____   _____

STEP 4

I will pursue the following new interests. (List at least four, with start deadlines of every three months over the next year.)

_____   _____

_____   _____

I will take these steps to get in touch with men from my past or men I've seen and always wondered about. (List three men and contact strategies for the coming year.)

_____

_____

_____

When I spot or meet a man who might be interesting to me, the following are some things I would feel comfortable doing to get or maintain his attention. (List at least three.)

_____

_____

_____

STEP 5

After a few casual conversations, I will know that he might be compatible if the following are true. (List five things about his behavior or background that will give you a good idea that you are suited for one another.)

_____   _____

_____   _____

_____   _____

After a few casual conversations, I will know I should *not* pursue this man further if he does the following. (List five things about his behavior or background that will give you a good idea that you're not a good match.)

_____   _____

_____   _____

_____   _____

The following are some types of men that are attractive to me (e.g., older, younger, or bachelors). (List the type(s) and describe why they are attractive to you.)

_____

_____

_____

Step 6

In order to get ready for sexual intimacy, I need to take the following steps to prepare my home. (List as many items as you can think of.)

_____	_____
_____	_____
_____	_____
_____	_____
_____	_____
_____	_____

In order to get ready for sexual intimacy, I need to take the following steps to prepare me. (List as many items as you can think of.)

_____	_____
_____	_____

_____   _____

_____   _____

_____   _____

_____   _____

Step 7

I will know the relationship is moving in the right direction when the following happen. (List many things that would please you about a relationship.)

_____   _____

_____   _____

_____   _____

_____   _____

_____   _____

_____   _____

The following are the things I will enjoy most about his family, friends, and living environment. (List at least four.)

_____   _____

_____   _____

The following are the things I will enjoy least about his family, friends, and living environment. (List at least four.)

_____   _____

_____   _____

I will take the following actions to increase my enjoyment and alleviate the issues just described. (List at least four.)

_____   _____

_____   _____

STEP 8

If I get disappointed that things don't happen the way I planned, I will remind myself of the following. (Show us your attitude here!)

_____

_____

_____

The following are the attitudes that I have going for me, or will soon acquire, as I tackle all steps.

_____

_____

_____

With the help of a lot of dynamic and successful ladies, we offer the ideas and provide a map. But only you can make the plan and take the action. When it comes to relationships with men, there are no one right way and no "must do" or "must not do." There are only good examples and solid suggestions waiting to be stamped with your own imprint and put into action with your own special style. At the fifty-plus stage of life, you get to make your own rules. Finally!

References

Brown, Helen Gurley. *Having It All: Love, Success, Sex, Money.* New York: Pocket Books, 1982.

Gauthier, Anne H., and Timothy M. Smeeding. "Patterns of Time Use of People Age 55 to 64 Years Old." Aging Studies Program Paper Series of the Maxwell School, Center for Policy Research, Syracuse University, March 2000.

Katz, Marc Evan. *I Can't Believe I'm Buying This Book: A Commonsense Guide to Successful Internet Dating.* Berkeley, Calif.: Ten Speed Press, 2003.

Kaye, Beverly L. *Up Is Not the Only Way: A Guide to Developing Workforce Talent,* 2nd edition. Palo Alto, Calif.: Davies-Black, 1997.

Sheehy, Gail. *New Passages: Mapping Your Life Across Time.* New York: Random House, 1995.

Taylor, Shelley E. *The Tending Instinct: Women, Men, and the Biology of Our Relationships.* New York: Henry Holt & Co., 2002.

Treasurer, Bill. *The Right Risk: Ten Powerful Principles for Taking Giant Leaps with Your Life.* San Francisco: Berrett-Koehler Publishers, 2003.

About the Authors

KATHERINE ELISE CHADDOCK is a university professor who enjoys writing not only for scholars, but also for regular consumers of good ideas and good reading. Her work, covering topics from strong single women to motherhood, investments, and romantic weekend getaways, has appeared in *Working Woman, Good Housekeeping, American Way, Parents, Washington Post Sunday Magazine, Washingtonian Magazine,* and other publications. She is also the author of four books on various aspects of American history. A graduate of Northwestern University School of Journalism, she holds a master's degree from the University of Southern California and a Ph.D. from the University of Utah. Katherine is a two-time divorcée and the mother of twenty-one-year-old twins. She lives in Charleston, South Carolina, where her recreational pursuits include tennis, kayaking, and lounging in the hammock.

EMILIE CHADDOCK EGAN holds a B.S. from Northwestern University and a J.D. from Northwestern University School of Law. She has logged many miles as a marathon runner; as a hockey, tennis, and soccer mom to her three now-grown children; and as a community volunteer and Junior Leaguer. In her varied career Emilie has worked as a telephone operator, an attorney, and an optician. She moved from Chicago to the mountains of Colorado to renew her spirit after her husband was killed while on a commercial bicycle tour. In addition to writing and working part-time, Emilie hikes, skis, snowshoes, golfs, and makes frequent visits to her children and grandchildren in Chicago, New York, and Denver.

Index